WALKING THE JURASSIC COAST

DORSET AND EAST DEVON:
THE WALKS, THE ROCKS, THE FOSSILS

By Ronald Turnbull

CICERONE

JUNIPER HOUSE, MURLEY MOSS,
OXENHOLME ROAD, KENDAL, CUMBRIA LA9 7RL
www.cicerone.co.uk

© Ronald Turnbull 2015
First edition 2015
ISBN: 978 1 85284 741 8
Reprinted 2017 and 2019 (with updates)

Printed in Singapore by KHL Printing
A catalogue record for this book is available from the British Library.

All photographs are by the author.

Updates to this Guide

Front cover: Layered Bridport Sandstone at East Cliff (Walk 13)

CONTENTS

Route symbols on OS map extracts
(for OS legend see printed OS maps)

	route
	shortcut
(person)	start/finish point
(person)	start point
(person)	finish point
(arrow)	route direction
(ammonite)	geological explanation point
(ammonite)	geological museum

Features on the overview map

(R)	Red Bed Roundabout (Chapter 1)
(P)	Purbeck Circuit (Chapter 5)
- - - -	County boundary
(shape)	Urban area

	400m
	200m
	75m
	0m

GPX files

GPX files for all routes can be downloaded for free at www.cicerone.co.uk/741/GPX.

Acknowledgements

Thanks to DG Turnbull, my base in the West Country; and to Dr Ian West of Southampton University, whose huge and detailed website was much of my grounding in the geology of the Wessex Coast. That coastline moves inexorably inland; in so doing it provides a vivid re-enactment of events of 100 million years ago, but also a lot of trouble for the footpath rangers of Devon and Dorset councils and the National Trust. All walkers must appreciate their useful and unobtrusive work.

You can't walk far on this coast without seeing that the sea was once full of ammonites. Today, not one ammonite (or belemnite or plesiosaur) lives on this planet. All were wiped out by the Earth's fifth great extinction event, the comet impact of 65 million years ago. Some geologists have already identified the sixth great extinction as being right now: caused not by a comet from the outer solar system, but by us. This walking book won't contain any preachy stuff about global warming, but it's dedicated to the environmentalists, scientists, occasional politicians, and many ordinary people trying to do something about it.

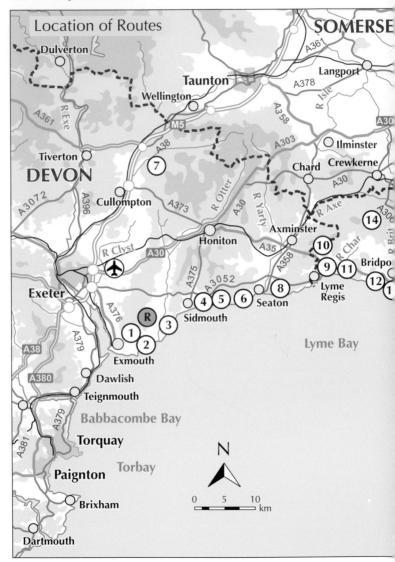

Location of Routes

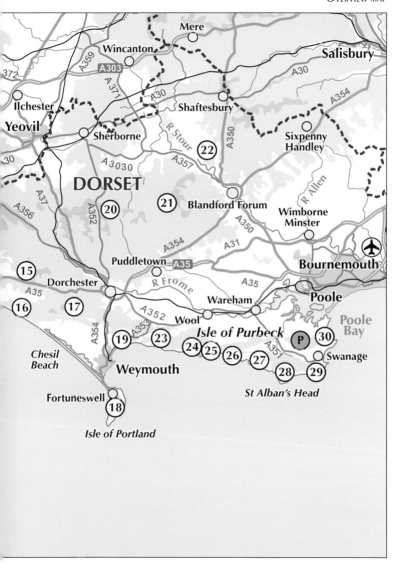

Strata of the Jurassic Coast

A quick guide to rock layers of the Jurassic Coast, youngest at the top. See also the diagram at the start of each walk and fuller explanation of strata in Appendix F.

sand & shingle	
Agglestone Grit	Tertiary: Agglestone Grit
CHALK	Chalk
GREENSAND	Greensand
GREENSAND	Greensand + unconformity
WEALDEN clay	lower Cretaceous: Wealden clay
PURBECK	Purbeck Limestone (Cretaceous/Jurassic)
PORTLAND	Jurassic: Portland Stone and Portland Sand
Kimmeridge Clay	Jurassic: Kimmeridge Clay
CORALLIAN	Jurassic: Corallian
OXFORD Clay	Jurassic: Oxford Clay
middle Jurassic / Forest Marble	Middle Jurassic: sandstone, clay (incl Forest Marble)
Inferior Oolite / Bridport Sands	Jurassic: Bridport Sands (and Inferior Oolite)
upper Lias	Jurassic: upper/middle Lias: sandstone, clay
Charmouth Mdstn	Jurassic: Charmouth Mudstone
BLUE LIAS	Jurassic: Blue Lias
PENARTH Group	Triassic: Penarth Group
MERCIA Mudstn	Triassic: Mercia Mudstone
OTTER Sandstone	Triassic: Otter Sandstone
B S Pebble Beds	Budleigh Salterton Pebble Bed
Aylesbeare Mdstn	Triassic: Aylsbeare Mudstone

Ammonite and Houns Tout from Chapman's Pool (Walk 28)

GEOLOGICAL TOPICS FEATURED ON THE WALKS		
Topic	Description	Walk no
Pebblebed Heath	moors lie on ancient riverbed pebbles	1
Budleigh Salterton Pebbles	outwash pebbles from a vanished mountain range	2
Otter Sandstone	red desert dunes, stream beds and tree roots	3
Sidmouth Red Beds	desert dunes and lake beds	4
Greensand at Salcombe Mouth	green glauconite mineral and fossil clams	4
Gypsum at Weston Mouth and Branscombe Mouth	dried-out desert salt lakes	5
Beer Stone and Beer Head Limestone	shelly limestone at the base of the chalk	6
Fossilised sea floor	former sea beds with shrimp burrows	6
Bindon Landslip	the Undercliff landslide of 1839	8
The Cobb	the Great Unconformity, and Portland Screw fossils underfoot	8
Monmouth Beach	ammonites, and the Lias layering	8
Mary Anning and Elizabeth Philpot	the all-time top fossil finder and her friend, from Lyme Regis	9
Black Ven	ammonites	9
Golden Cap: Boulder Arcs	signs of long-ago cliff collapse	10
Tsunami of 1755	the UK's second-worst tidal wave preserved in beach shingle	11
Seatown Summary	the Great Unconformity, ammonites and belemnites	11
Symondsbury's Inferior Oolite	shells, ammonites, belemnites and red snuff-box concretions	12
Shutes Lane	a Dorset hollow way	12
Eype's Mouth and Fault Corner	a fault plane and its effects on the landscape	12

GEOLOGICAL TOPICS FEATURED ON THE WALKS		
Topic	**Description**	**Walk no**
Burton Cliff and East Cliff	Lias layering in the Bridport Sands	13
Greensand Summits	Devon and Dorset's Greensand plateau	14
Flint and Chert	flint from the chalk rocks, chert from the Greensand	15
Oolite limestone	tropical limestone sand makes great Dorset buildings	16
Chesil Beach	longshore drift forms 29km of pebble beach	16
The Portland Roach	the Portland top layer with the 'Portland Screw' fossils	18
Osmington Doggers	metre-wide limestone spheroids	19
Redcliff Point	Oxford Clay and ammonites	19
Chalk Fossils	shells and an uncommon Cretaceous ammonite	20
Chalk Escarpment at Bulbarrow	Dorset's chalk plateau	21
Ham and Portland	Dorset's two special stones for building	21
The Durdle Wall: Portland and Purbeck Erect	cliffs crumpled by the Alpine mountain building	24
Fossil Forest	tree shapes preserved in algal slime	25
Mupe Bay and Wealden Clay	Lake-bed clay forms bays and a valley; carbonised tree fragments	26
Making clay at Kimmeridge Bay	rocks as they are forming: crushed ammonites, dolomite stones expanding underground	27
Chapman's Pool	oysters, ammonites and four sorts of boulders	28
Purbeck Marble	preserved snailbeds make cathedrals of England	29
Dancing Ledge	ammonites and chert	29

Seabed ripples in Portland Stone, above Mutton Cove (Walk 18)

INTRODUCTION

Durdle Door (Walk 24)

Down at the seaside – and up on the downs. Dorset and South Devon have sweeping sea cliffs, magnificent rock architecture and hidden coves. Inland are long green ridgeways. Gentle grassland, the big sea view, and the ramparts of an Iron Age settlement make an easier morning before the strenuousness sea-level to cliff top of the coastal afternoon. And at day's end, a swim in the sea, a cold drink, and perhaps another ice cream.

It's not, however, the ice creams (splendid as they are) that make this 160km of coastline into one of only three 'natural heritage' World Sites in the UK. (The others are the Giant's Causeway coast and St Kilda; while Hadrian's Wall, Stonehenge etc are 'cultural'.) It's not just the windswept

downland, or the crashing waves below, the long views across the water, or the thyme and trefoil of the meadow slopes. The clue to the coastline's World Heritage status is contained in the name. The varied rock formations of this short coastline, the chalk and limestone and red sandstone and shale, tell a 200-million-year story that's not just the Jurassic but the later Cretaceous and earlier Trias too.

So while these small-hill and seaside walks are enjoyable in themselves, you're missing out if you don't also spare an eye for various events of the Dinosaur times: the quartzite pebbles of Budleigh Salterton, washed by flash floods out of a mountain range somewhere to the south where today we see only the sea; tree trunks of 150 million

15

Middle Bottom, on the chalk coast west of Lulworth Cove (Walk 24)

years ago at Lulworth Cove; the soupy Cretaceous sea that carved its way right across England; ammonites the size of dinner plates at Dancing Ledge; the crumple zone caused by Italy's continuing impact with Europe.

Earth science can be heavy going. It takes a hand lens, a hammer and half a lifetime to distinguish the 70 different ammonite zones of Lyme Regis. However, the Jurassic Coast is not just a rock garden, but a rock kindergarten. This is the place to see the spectacular events of 200 million years ago; to understand what was going on; to see and touch the fossils and rock forms that make us believe in sliding continents, and million-year cycles of the moon, ice ages and sudden drownings of the sea.

The routes in this book are not geology field trips. They are meant to be enjoyed, first and foremost, as

walks. The rock facts, and pictures to go with them, are additional extras. If you don't feel like stuffing your head with science, you can just stride out with the wind in your hair, over another green cliff top and along another overhanging chalkface, and then down for tea and scones and a swim in the sea.

THE JURASSIC COAST

In geological terms, the Jurassic Coast is a misnomer – it's just as much Triassic and Cretaceous. But in walking terms, the coast between Exmouth in Devon and Dorset's Poole Bay offers spectacular coastline and cliffs rising to 191m at Golden Cap, in combination with grassy downland inland, often itself with great sea views. Many of the walks combine these two landscapes. A few of them are entirely inland: one in Devon and six in Dorset. Up on the downland, you can stride out without thinking too much about the underlying rock forms or attempting to spot any fossils.

For the ambitious, two full-day outings are also recommended, and marked on the overview map at the front of this guide. The Red Bed Roundabout (33km and about 10 hours) is summarised in Chapter 1 and the Isle of Purbeck Circuit (about 27.5km and 8 hours) is summarised in Chapter 5.

The full 100 mile **Jurassic Coast Path** from Exmouth to Poole Harbour is a very rewarding extended walk. Almost all of it is covered by walks in this book.

High summer, the last week in July to the end of August, is convenient in that the Lulworth Ranges are open throughout the week, but being the school holidays this is the busiest time of all on the beaches and in villages. May and June are quieter, and the climate is slightly cooler – just arrange any Lulworth walking over a weekend. September can also be good, with cooler air but the sea still warm.

The winter season (November to March) may have rain and storms, and mud underfoot; accommodation can be closed and the baggage transfer service not in operation. However, with a slightly higher level of determination and equipment the walks can also be enjoyed in the off-season, and winter is the top time for fossil finding!

GETTING THERE AND AROUND

The West Country is the UK's busiest holiday destination. Its rail and road links with the rest of the country are fast and efficient, but can become uncomfortably crowded at the peak holiday period of late July and throughout August, and in particular

East Hill, descending to Osmington (Walk 19)

the bank holiday at the last weekend of August. Motorways, trunk roads within the area and seaside car parks can all be congested.

For air travellers, local airports at Exeter and Bournemouth serve the rest of the UK; slightly further away, Bristol has a better range of overseas connections. However, the very good rail links make London airports the convenient touchdown point.

The rail system links into the area at Exeter (with branch line to Exmouth), Honiton, Axminster, Dorchester (with branch to Weymouth), Wool and Wareham, and across Poole Harbour at Poole and Bournemouth. The 'Jurassic Coast' buses link many of the coastal villages with each other and with Exeter and the other rail stations.

On the Dorset coast www. dorsetforyou.gov.uk has detailed bus stop information. The public transport journey planner is at www.travelinesw. com or Traveline SW app. The official Jurassic Coast site is at www.jurassic-coast.org, covering Devon as well as Dorset, and includes some information on transport.

STAYING THE NIGHT

The Devon coast has a succession of small towns, all with good facilities and communications: Exmouth, Budleigh Salterton, Sidmouth, Seaton/ Beer, continuing into Dorset with Lyme Regis and Bridport. The main Dorset part of our coast, by contrast, has two large towns, Weymouth and Swanage, but between them quieter coastlines, with smaller villages where accommodation and shops are quite limited.

A good listing of walker-friendly accommodation on and close to the coastal path is at www. luggagetransfers.co.uk (who also provide baggage transport to long-distance path walkers). Accommodation and general tourist information are found at www.visitdevon.co.uk and www.visit-dorset.com. The site www. jurassiccoast.org, covering Devon as well as Dorset, also has some information on accommodation.

MAPS AND GPS

The coast footpath itself is clear and well waymarked, but the inland sections of the walks in this book are less clear. The best mapping is the Ordnance Survey Explorer at 1:25,000 scale, which marks field boundaries. The double-sided OL15 (Purbeck and South Dorset) covers all the coastal walks from Bridport eastwards. Other walks require sheets OL20, 115, 116 and 117, as indicated in the walks headers.

A compass is a very useful aid in low cloud or across pathless fields, even if your skills only extend to 'northwest, southeast' rather than precision bearings. Magnetic deviation is about 0.5° west (2018). This can safely be ignored. GPS receivers should be set to the British National Grid (known

On Golden Cap (Walks 10 & 11), looking east to Thorncombe Beacon

variously as British Grid, Ord Srvy GB, BNG, or OSGB GRB36). A set of GPX files for the routes in this guide can be downloaded from www.cicerone. co.uk/741/GPX.

The excellent geological mapping of the British Geological Survey is more than most readers of this book will need. If you want them, the sheets are 350 Torquay (Walk 1 only), 339 (Newton Abbot), 326/340 (Sidmouth), 327 (Bridport), 342 (Weymouth), 343 Swanage. Simpler coverage of the bedrock is on the free and very useful iGeology app for iPhone, Android and Kindle. Given an internet connection it will home in on your current location or any placename. Also very useful is the cliff section diagram from the *Official Guide to the Jurassic Coast*, which diagrams the whole coast in a strip 3m (yes, that's 10ft) long and in much greater detail than the sketches

in Appendix G. The cliff sections can be cut from that book and carried in a map case.

Any walk along this coast will pass a recent cliff collapse sooner or later. You may see holidaymakers relaxing at the cliff foot; geologists, however, are more aware of the processes of coastal change. They wear hard hats and approach the cliff foot for brief periods only, while taking their lunch break well out on the beach.

If you should come across a recent and dangerous cliff fall, inform the Coastguard on 999, or the County Council: Devon 0345 155 1004, or Dorset 01305 224463.

What can catch geologists, preoccupied with an intriguing bit of rock, is the tide. Always be aware of whether the tide is going out or coming in, and the times of high tides. If you're cut off by the tide, or see others in difficulties, dial 999 and ask for the Coastguard.

TIDES ON THE INTERNET

Tide tables for dozens of coastal harbours and up to a year ahead are at www.visitmyharbour. com. Note that times are given in GMT, so add 1hr for British Summer Time.

Specifically geological risks arise from clambering about on unstable Jurassic cliffs and landslips, and from hammering at rocks without wearing goggles – early geologist Adam Sedgwick lost an eye that way, and Mary Anning of Lyme Regis lost her pet dog in a landslip.

Range warning sign, Lulworth. Some first-class walking through the tank ranges is open only during the summer holiday season or at weekends, see Walks 25 and 26

Devon and Dorset lanes are narrow with high hedges. The normal advice is to walk on the right, facing oncoming traffic, but it's often better to stick to the outside of any bend, whether left or right, to see and be seen.

USING THIS GUIDE

The times in the walk headers are for a moderate-paced walker (an hour for 4km, plus 12 minutes for every 100m of ascent). If you get interested in the rocks and fossils this can add 2 hours to any walk. The headers also mention any issues with tides, or with the Lulworth Ranges. Every year, one or two sections of the coastal footpath will be temporarily closed due to landslips: check at local information centres or on the South West Coast Path website www.southwestcoastpath. com – search for 'route changes' in the top menus.

The route headers include a mini-guide to the rock layers underfoot: for details see Appendix F. The wavy break under the Greensand indicates the 'Great Unconformity' described below. A small ammonite marker on the route maps (see the map key at the front of this guide) shows points that have geological notes in the text. A green ammonite marks indoor geology, museums where your beach ammonites are complemented with plesiosaurs, and other rarer finds – these are listed in Appendix B.

GEOLOGICAL INTRODUCTION

Old Harry (sea stack) at daybreak from Studland beach (Walk 30)

THE SEA

The insight that starts off geology – Aristotle wondered about it, and so did Leonardo da Vinci – is that rocks such as sandstone really are the remains of other earlier rocks, broken down and recycled over immense periods of time. What breaks them down can be rain or wind, streams or rivers, or even ice. But the main sand-maker is the sea. Almost all of the rocks of the Jurassic Coast are 'sedimentary'. There are no igneous rocks, arriving red hot and fresh from volcanoes or congealing deep underground. There are no metamorphic ones, cooked and mangled by mountain-building. What we see are sandstones, which are made of sand, and limestones, directly dumped on the sea bed by chemical precipitation.

When we look at a rock, what we want to know is: where did it come from, how was it made? How convenient, then, that every coastal walk has cliff face exposures and beautifully polished pebbles. But also, working away right here in the present day, the same geological earth force that made the limestone and sandstone in the first place – the sea.

The sea nibbles into the land along a narrow band between the high and the low tide lines: it's like a strimmer slicing into a tangle of weeds. And so at low tide the shoreline often shows a wave-cut platform; rock beds cut off almost flat, between the minus 10m contour and the zero one, the only zone where the waves can actually attack.

Broad Bench, Hobarrow Bay (Walk 26) – a fine example of a wave-cut platform

At the cliff base, the waves start by grinding out a notch. It's sand and small pebbles that act as the abrasive. When the cliff is sufficiently undercut, down it comes. The rubble on the beach protects the cliff face for a time. But straight away the finer dust and sand are carried away: from above you see them staining the sea. The smaller pebbles go next. A century later, only an arc of big sea boulders, seen from the cliff top above (see Walk 10), marks the site of a former cliff collapse.

Wherever a faultline has already weakened the rockface, the waves cut inwards: and now a new and surprising cave-making agent takes over. Sand-scrubbing isn't effective within a hollow. Instead, the incoming wave compresses air within the cracks of the rock. As the wave sucks, the air expands, almost explosively, driving the rock apart.

And so a small hollow becomes a big hole – look in the roof of any sea cave and you should see the faultline that provided the initial point of weakness. Where a faultline passes right through a headland, sea-caves at either end join to become an arch. The arch collapses to form a sea stack. Wave action attacks the base of the stack; it falls; and the sea moves on inland.

THE GREAT UNCONFORMITY

Will this process of sea erosion, given time, eventually erase the whole of England? We know it will – because it already did! In the Cretaceous (the Chalk time), a soupy, algae-infested sea carved its way right across an

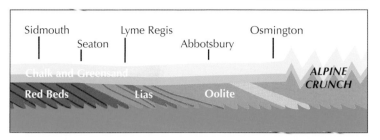

Sidmouth   Lyme Regis   Osmington
   Seaton   Abbotsbury

Chalk and Greensand   **ALPINE CRUNCH**

Red Beds   **Lias**   **Oolite**

The Great Unconformity: chalk and Greensand above red mudstone, Weston Cliff (Walk 4)

old content of red sandstone and layered limestone. Along 50 miles of the Jurassic Coast, between Budleigh Salterton and White Nothe, the Greensand and Chalk which were the bed of that soupy sea slice clean across the older beds, chopping off the tops of the older (Triassic and Jurassic) rocks. At any one place (Golden Cap, say) it just looks as if the Chalk sits on top of other rocks in the ordinary way. It's over several walks,

or in the cliff diagram at the back of this book, that you appreciate that the Chalk doesn't just sit on the earlier rocks, but actually cuts across them.

An unconformity is where one rock sits on the eroded down remains of an earlier one, implying a time-gap of missing rocks between. The unconformity at the base of the Chalk Sea can be traced from Hampshire to Devon: it's known as the Great Unconformity.

23

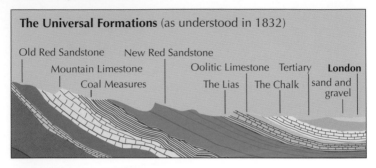

The Universal Formations (as understood in 1832)

Old Red Sandstone   New Red Sandstone
    Mountain Limestone   Oolitic Limestone   Tertiary   **London**
        Coal Measures   The Lias   The Chalk   sand and
                                    gravel

THE UNIVERSAL FORMATIONS

Geology started in England – specifically in the Jurassic limestones and sandstones around Bath. Around 1795 a surveyor called William Smith, with access to coal mines and canals, began to make sense of what was what and in what order. And the first thing was several major layers of stone that happened all over the place. The Chalk stretches from Beer and Old Harry Rocks by way of the Wiltshire Downs to the coast of Yorkshire. The New Red Sandstone, as seen all along the Devon end of the Jurassic Coast, is seen again in Cheshire, and under Nottingham

Castle. And underneath the New Red is where you come across the coal.

The Universal Formations are not in fact worldwide. But the Coal Measures, the New Red Sandstone and the Lias are big, recognisable slabs of stone that do indeed reach a long way sideways. The NRS is identified from North Africa to Greenland. Nature wanted to make it easy for those first geologists. Straight away they could start to work out what was what – in a way that was useful, too. If Lord Egremont's land was the Old Red Sandstone, there was no point at all in Lord Egremont digging into it in

Sea stacks at Ladram Bay (Walk 3). Devon's Red Beds are part of the New Red Sandstone that stretches to Cheshire, Southern Scotland, and even Greenland

the hope of coal: the Coal Measures lie on top of the Old Red.

Modern geology has abandoned these ancient classifications. But for beginners, whether in the 18th century or today, they're jolly useful. The Jurassic Coast involves the New Red Sandstone in the west, the Lias of Lyme Regis (and also of north Somerset, Glamorgan, and Yorkshire), and, of course, the Chalk.

THE FOSSILS

When it comes to the detail, Nature again goes out of her way to be helpful. Sedimentary layers, such as those of the Jurassic Coast, contain the remains of the creatures that lived in them. God clearly wants geologists: fossils are preserved in half a dozen different ways.

Calcite – the mineral that forms most seashells – is itself extremely persistent and can survive for 200 million years embedded in the sand. Alternatively, the original mineral (fishbone, say) can be replaced, an atom at a time, with a rock mineral such as golden-black pyrites. Sometimes the rocks preserve the hole where a fossil was: this could be a shrimp burrow, or it could be the footprint of a dinosaur. Pure carbon is as persistent as calcite; and around Lulworth you'll see bits of trees turned into smears of coal. More exotic forms of preservation – amber, opal – are very rare, but can save quick-rotting insects in the minutest detail.

And so, for all the component layers within, say, the Lias, William Smith was able to work out three very useful principles (see below). Using these principles, today's geologists identify 71 different rock layers at Lyme Regis, each with a slightly different ammonite. And us amateurs can

Ammonites below Golden Cap (Walks 10–12)

- If rock layers in two places are the same sort of stone (gritty limestone, say) representing the same sort of sea bed, but have different sets of fossils, then they're different rocks.
- Once it's gone, it doesn't come back. If two rock layers look different but have the same fossils in them, then they're the same rock layer.
- And if there aren't any fossils at all, then look at the layer just above or the one just below.

Upper Greensand shell below Higher Dunscombe Cliff (Walk 4)

do the same thing on a larger scale. Find ammonites, and you're probably in the Jurassic – though they didn't become completely extinct until the end of the Cretaceous (chalk) period. The giant ammonites (Titanites) put you at the very top of the Jurassic, in the Portland Stone. The 'Portland Screw' puts you even more precisely in the Portland Stone's top layer. The bent oysters nicknamed the Devil's Toenails only lie in the Lias. And right outside the Coastal Heritage Centre at Charmouth, a beautiful rugose coral puts you firmly in the Carboniferous Period – yes, someone's been building sea defences out of a Wrong Sort of Rock.

Along the Jurassic Coast, you will find fossils. What you won't find are giant reptiles and fish, or the beautiful round ammonites you see in museums. They're in museums precisely because they're rare and wonderful. What you will find – and what I've mostly tried to show you in this book – are broken bits, stuff that's been washed over by the sea, plus plenty of seashells, and (once you've got your eye in) worm burrows and algal slime. Your first ammonite could take ten minutes, or it could take ten days. It's a thrilling moment either way.

Your chances are better away from car parks and people. They're better at dawn after an overnight high tide; in autumn and winter; and especially after a winter storm. There's no need to carry a hammer – over much of this coast, hammering for fossils is illegal. A magnifying glass can help, but the best bits of equipment are feet and eyeballs. Look at clean, sea-washed boulders; also at shaly, friable sort of rock, especially where it's

COLLECTING FOSSILS

Fossils washed onto the beach will be lost to the sea unless someone collects them. On the other hand, irresponsible collecting spoils the fun for others and can destroy real scientific value.

- Collecting of loose specimens from beach and foreshore is acceptable over almost all of the Jurassic Coast.
- Use of hammers, chisels and other hard tools is deprecated or banned over much of the Jurassic Coast. Digging into cliffs is discouraged (and can be dangerous).
- Byelaws forbid removal of pebbles from Budleigh Salterton beach and Chesil Beach.
- Don't collect more than you need: if you find two, leave one for somebody else.
- Any important finds can be reported to the Charmouth Heritage Centre via www.charmouth.org/chcc.

The full fossil code for West Dorset is at www.charmouth.org/chcc.

freshly broken open. Glance along the pebbles turned over by the latest high tide. Recent cliff falls are tempting, but they are also dangerous. If sitting down, sift through some shingle or sand with your fingers. And life of 250 million years ago is all around you.

THE DRIFT OF THE CONTINENTS

How come the New Red Sandstone, all over the UK, appears in the time just on top of all the coal? What's the cause of the chalk, arriving everywhere just above the Lias but not at all before or after? William Smith didn't know why – but we do.

It all fits into the theory that at one point the Earth's continents were clumped together in a single mass called Pangaea – and that since then (and indeed before then) they've been wandering around the earth's surface like students on the gap year. Originally just a matter of scissors and an atlas and fitting Africa against South America, the theory is verified by matching the rocks, and the fossils; also by traces of magnetism no longer pointing north because of the continents' wanderings. The way America is still drifting away west at 5cm a year has even been measured directly with GPS.

The coal measures formed when they did because, just then, the bit we call England was drifting across the equator and was a soggy coastal rainforest. The red sands that came afterwards were when we'd carried on north a bit, to the tropic zone that now holds

The coastline from Ladram Bay to Beer

the Sahara and the Gobi Desert. And at this very moment Italy is a slow-motion car crash into the rest of Europe, shoving up the Alps and, in a small way, the corner of Lulworth Cove.

EASTWARDS IS ALSO 'UP'

Reading the 'Jurassic' Coast west to east, from Devon to Dorset and Poole Harbour, is also reading from oldest rocks to younger ones: in geological terms, from bottom to top. The first, and lowest, of the great Universal Formations to show along the coastline is the New Red Sandstone – the 'Red Beds' that stretch from Exmouth along the Devon coast to Salcombe Mouth, just short of the Dorset border.

On top of them lies the stripy Lias of Lyme Regis, with its sea monsters and ammonites. Eastwards and upwards from Lyme, it's the oolite, the limestone sands of a semi-tropical beach paradise a bit like the Bahamas. Eastwards again it's the Chalk: but because of that Great Unconformity, the Chalk is also on top of everything else, all the way back west again to Sidmouth.

The introduction to each of the book's five sections explains why its particular sort of stone formed at its particular time in the east–west sequence of the Devon-Dorset coastline. Within the actual walks we'll be seeing the pebbles sandblasted by the desert winds, the sea creatures preserved in the stones, the rocks raised upright by Italy's arrival. At the end of the book, Appendix E is a quick timechart of all eleven geological periods, for when we can't quite remember what did come after the Carboniferous, marked with the main earth-shaking events affecting Dorset. Appendix F is a detailed layout, bottom to top, of the main Jurassic Coast rocks. Finally there's a coloured in cliff diagram, all the way along.

The guys at UNESCO got it right. Prepare for swamps and coral seas, flash floods and earthquakes, sea monsters and non-existent mountains, over 100 miles, and 200 million years, of English seaside.

1 DEVON'S RED BEDS

- Budleigh Salterton Pebbles
- Red Otter Sandstone
- Red Mercia Mudstone at Sidmouth and Seaton
- The Great Unconformity
- Landslipped chalk at Beer
- Hartridge Greensand plateau

Otter Sandstone in the foreground and lower cliff, Mercia Mudstone above, with a glimpse of the yellow Greensand that cuts across the clifftop (Walk 4)

INTRODUCTION

About 350 million years ago, the world's moving land masses assembled themselves into a single supercontinent called Pangaea. The bit we now call Britain found itself about 20° north of the equator, deep in the middle of the continent. Far from any ocean, it was in the wash-out zone of a great mountain range (the Variscan) formed when the Pangaea continent crunched together.

Today, 20° north is the zone of the Sahara and the Gobi, and it was the same back in the Triassic Period. The sands of one great desert form the New Red Sandstone rocks of southeast Devon; and they're also in what were then the lands alongside, since separated by the opening Atlantic: Mexico, Greenland and North America.

Sea cliffs from Exmouth to Axmouth show the swirly patterns of desert dunes. You'll also see the more intricate patterns of sandbanks in seasonal desert streams, and the pebble beds left by flash floods. There are dried out desert lakes, like the salt lakes of Death Valley today.

Deserts aren't noted for their wildlife; what you won't see in the Red Beds are fossils. Traces remain of some scrubby trees. Dinosaurs did pass through; their footprints and occasional remains are in the local museums. But for abundant life seen in the cliffs and pebbles, you'll have to move on eastwards, into the Jurassic Period.

Flint houses, Beer (Walk 6)

WALK 1
Budleigh Salterton and Woodbury Castle

Start/Finish	East Budleigh SY 065 848
Distance	19km (11 miles)
Ascent	300m (1000ft)
Approx time	5¼hrs
Terrain	tracks and paths
Maps	Explorer 115 Exmouth; Landranger 192 Exeter
Parking	(free) off Hayes Lane just south of East Budleigh church; also Woodbury Castle SY 032 872

The red-stained and ancient pebbles of Budleigh's sea cliff were washed down out of a mountain range that's now completely vanished away. They will easily distract any geologist from the (equally reddish-pink and rounded) human body-parts on the nudist beach below them.

Inland, the pebbles make a rather hopeless building material, or decorative cobblestone pavements. They also make a series of barren heathlands, linked together for the inland leg of this walk, which also takes in the ramparts of Woodbury Castle.

Head back on Hayes Lane to Sir Walter Raleigh pub, and turn up left to the gate into the churchyard. Pass round the church to a gate onto the lane beyond (Yettington Road).

Turn left, out of the village. The lane is narrow and nettly but little used. Pass the entrance gates to Clifton Rolle Estate, then (just before **Yettington**) turn right to follow an unsignposted lane. It rises north. After an informal parking area in woods the road dips, and bends right. Here take the bridleway track ahead.

Bear right on the main track to cross a footbridge beside a ford. The track runs uphill onto heathland. With a warning sign about the MoD Grenade Range seen ahead, turn right at a bridleway waymark. A rough path runs under trees, along the bottom edge of the heathland, with fields below the high hedge on the right.

> **MERCIA Mudstn**
> **OTTER Sandstone**
> **B S Pebble Beds**

The well-washed Budleigh Salterton pebbles show their proper off-white quartzite colour without the usual red-stained surface.

The path fords a stream. ◄ In another 100 metres it joins a wide, grassy track. Turn back sharp left (leaving the bridleway) to follow the track uphill through the heather of **Colaton Raleigh Common**. Firing range flagpoles and warning signs are on the left. Any red flags can be ignored as this track does not run into the firing range area. As the slope eases, the track joins a wider one coming up out of the firing range, to reach in 100 metres a track junction at the crest of the heathland ridge.

The route will now have East Devon Way markers as far as East Budleigh Common.

Turn left on this track, with bridleway markers, along the moorland crest through tall gorse. ◄ The track passes to left of a tree clump and into less gorsey ground. With the B3180 nearby on the right, the bridleway forks off right but keep ahead on the main track.

It runs down to bend left at a pine clump, and runs up towards the wooded summit of **Woodbury Castle**. Keep ahead up paths under open woodland to the ramparts of the hill fort.

Follow the ramparts round to the left, to a car park alongside **B3180**.

map continues on page 35

PEBBLEBED HEATH

Colaton Raleigh Common

The Budleigh Salterton Pebble Beds form the cliffs west of Budleigh Salterton. Quartzite pebbles are very tough: much tougher than the mudstone they're embedded in. So over much of the high ground above the Otter Valley the red mudstone has eroded away to leave just the pebbles, up to 30m deep. In the same way, at High Peak and elsewhere, chalk has eroded away leaving just its flints. Although formed in a completely different way, the quartzite pebbles are the same silica mineral as flint and chert.

The pebble beds make for well-drained, acidic soils. After Bronze Age tree clearance the soils have been mostly washed away, to leave the dry, infertile heathland today. Unfarmable and abandoned, they now form the Pebblebed Heaths series of nature reserves.

Woody, a reproduction Rhynchosaur as found at Ladram Bay in 1993, is occasionally spotted roaming on Woodbury Common. Slightly less elusive is the Dartford warbler, once almost extinct, making its comeback across these commons.

The route continues below this car park, but first cross the road and pass through more parking areas to a viewpoint board.

Woodbury Castle scarp with views over to the River Exe and Dartmoor

You are at the edge of the **Pebblebed escarpment** – the plinth of the interpretation board is made of Budleigh Salterton pebbles. The ground ahead drops away steeply to the softer Aylesbeare Mudstones, the River Exe and distant Dartmoor.

The route follows the East Devon Way markers on the ground, but this is not the same as the EDW line on maps.

Return across the road, to find a path at the south end of the car park, with East Devon Way marker. ◄ The path heads downhill, south, crossing a lane near **Four Firs** into another car park. Pass through it to a gate and a wide, smooth track running uphill and through a strip of pines. At their far edge, keep ahead on a small path, eroded and pebbly, downhill. Here path erosion means you can inspect a soil profile of the pebblebed heaths. The path skirts around to left of a flooded quarry hole, then joins a wider track arriving from the left. This runs ahead, between quarried areas, and up into woods to a lane.

From here over **East Budleigh Common** to Squabmoor Reservoir there are many wandering paths. (Keeping roughly south will get you onto the track east of Squabmoor Reservoir; from the common you will see both the reservoir and the track to its left.) Cross the lane and keep to left of the parking area on a downhill path. After 200 metres fork right on a path over East Budleigh Common. It meets a track arriving from the right, to descend to a vehicle barrier and a small lane.

Cross onto an earth path descending into woods. At the slope foot, meet a stony track. Bear left on this, as it rises to run up to left of Squabmoor Reservoir. It runs downhill to join a lane near **Dalditch farm**.

Follow the lane ahead, bending slightly to the right, until you see a railway viaduct high ahead. Before reaching it turn up right, on a track marked 'permissive cycleway', to join the tarred cycle path. It bends up under tall spruce trees, to meet the tarmacked cycle path on the railbed.

You could divert left for the view from the viaduct. But this route turns right, following the railway path under two road bridges. To get onto the second of these, Castle Lane, either scramble up the bank on the left or continue for 200 metres to a signpost, where a cycle path heads back up left to join the lane.

Turn right (south) along Castle Lane, and where it bends right, keep ahead onto a wide earth path with footpath signpost for West

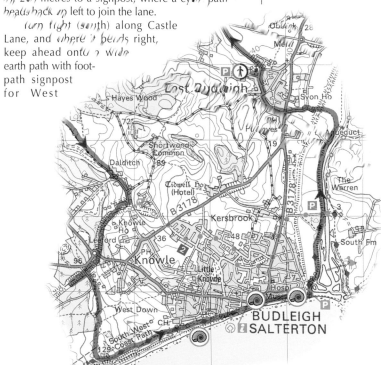

Littleham Cove to Budleigh Salterton and beyond

Down Beacon. The path emerges at the corner of a golf course. Keep ahead along the left edge of the golf for 200 metres, then bear right to a fingerpost. The path continues through scrubby woodland and gorse, to meet the coast path at the brink of high cliffs called **The Floors**.

The Pebblebed cliffs are 500 metres back to the right, see Walk 2.

Turn left on the cliff path, which descends gradually, soon in scrubby woodland. Various paths turn off left into **Budleigh Salterton**, but keep ahead on the main coast path down to the end of the shingle beach. ◀ Head along the esplanade, keeping below small seafront cliffs on the path behind beach huts (with some fossil tree roots behind them, see Walk 2).

If the wetland path is flooded, an alternative path runs north to the same lane. Continued to the east, the lane leads to a bridge over River Otter joining Walk 3.

At the village end turn left on a path around a car park to the Otter Estuary. The path follows the edge of the wetlands, past a bird hide, to a lane. ◀

Cross the lane to the continuing riverside path. Otter Sandstone is on the far bank, mixed dunes and flash flood deposits. After 1.2km, the metal Clamour Bridge is seen ahead. Just before reaching it, bear left on a footpath that crosses a concrete flood weir, then curves left on a raised flood embankment. The path becomes enclosed, then joins a track on its left to run out to the corner of a lane.

At this point, behind a large horse chestnut on the left, is an old barn The Pound built of Devon cob, a mix of straw and red mud.

Turn left, to the **B3178** at the Rolle Arms at the edge of East Budleigh. Cross into Lower Budleigh, which becomes Middle Street. ◀ Middle Street runs north, past the Drake School, to the end of Hayes Lane below the church. The car park is to the left up the lane.

WALK 2
Budleigh Salterton

Start/Finish	East Budleigh SY 065 848
Distance	12.5km (7½ miles)
Ascent	200m (650ft)
Approx time	3½hrs
Terrain	paths and tracks
Maps	Explorer 115 Exmouth; Landranger 192 Exeter
Parking	(free) off Hayes Lane, just south of East Budleigh church

Old lanes lead to a sudden arrival at the Floors cliff tops, with a return by Budleigh Salterton and River Otter. You miss out on the Pebblebed Heaths inland (Walk 1). This could allow time for the Pebblebed cliffs west of the village, the fossil desert floor of the Otter Sandstone, the plant root traces behind the beach huts, and Budleigh's thatched museum with its 450-million-year-old seashell. Not to mention a spot of sea bathing. If you have forgotten your swimsuit, the naturist area is below the Pebblebed cliffs.

Head back on Hayes Lane to Sir Walter Raleigh pub, and turn down right (High Street) to cross a bridge. The street continues with the stream on its left.

Opposite the Drake School turn right in a tarmac then concrete track through a farm. The track continues stony and hedged up a valley floor. At crossing tracks, continue ahead on the track marked 'no entry' – this is an 'unadopted road', hence the official road sign. The track, somewhat sunken, also does duty as a stream but gets drier as it rises.

After 800 metres from the 'no entry' signs, watch out for footpath signs on both sides of the track. Take the one on the left, through a metal kissing gate. The path has a high blackthorn hedge on its left to a stile. Across this the path rises over a hilltop (**Shortwood Common**) of bramble,

> **MERCIA Mudstn**
> **OTTER Sandstone**
> **B S Pebble Beds**

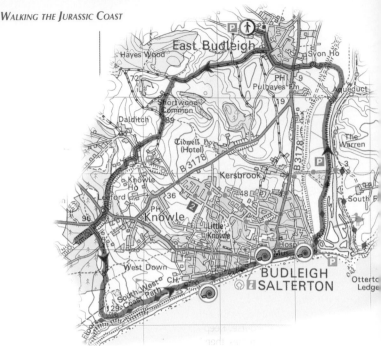

bracken and willow
herb as well as the dreaded
Himalayan balsam.

The path drops slightly to the corner of a sunken track. Keep ahead on this, over a low rise then down south for 200 metres. The main track now bends right and drops quite steeply, hollowed out into the soft red mudstone, which shows layers of unconsolidated silt between chunky layers of sandstone. ◄

The soft red mudstone does have a tendency to revert to soft red mud.

The track levels off to meet a lane, where you turn left towards a high viaduct. Before reaching it turn up right, on a track marked 'permissive cycleway'. It bends up under tall spruce trees, to meet the tarmacked cycle path on the railbed.

You could divert left for the view from the viaduct. But this route turns right, following the railway path under two road bridges. To get onto the second of these,

Desert soil surface with wind-scoured pebbles, Budleigh Salterton west beach

Castle Lane, either scramble up the bank on the left or continue for 200 metres to a signpost, where a cycle path heads back up left to join the lane.

Turn right (south) along Castle Lane, and where it bends right, keep ahead onto a wide earth path with footpath signpost for West Down Beacon. The path emerges at the corner of a golf course. Keep ahead along the left edge of the golf for 200 metres, then bear right to a fingerpost. The path continues through scrubby woodland and gorse, to meet the coast path at the brink of high cliffs called **The Floors**.

Turn left on the cliff path, which descends gradually, soon in scrubby woodland. Various paths turn off left into **Budleigh Salterton**, but keep ahead on the main coast path down to the end of the shingle beach. ▶ Head along the esplanade, keeping below small seafront cliffs on the path behind beach huts.

The very low cliff behind the huts shows **fossil tree roots** (rhizoconcretions). Some scrubby desert trees got their roots down into underground water below a seasonal stream bed. Calcite mineral deposited around these roots has preserved their shapes. A couple of the tree roots stand out from the red mudstone, with a clear air gap behind them.

The Pebblebed cliffs are 500 metres back to the right.

BUDLEIGH SALTERTON PEBBLES

At Budleigh Salterton, a whole cliff is made of potato-size pebbles out of mountains, now vanished, that stood where the English Channel now is. On the surface, the pebbles have the 'New Red' iron staining. But inside they're off-white, and very tough. It's the stone called quartzite: hard quartz sand, cemented together with the same quartz mineral. Others are exotic volcanics, greenish and blue-grey. These stones are altogether un-English, and resemble the rocks of Brittany.

The pebbles look their best wetted with seawater on the beach below. A selection is also in Budleigh's small thatched museum, and one of those has broken open to reveal a small seashell. The pebbles are much older than the Red Bed rock they're embedded in, and this fossil is more than twice as old as any of the others along England's south coast; its eventful life started in the shallow fringes of the Tornquist Sea, which lay as far south as today's Australia, about 440 million years ago in the Ordovician period.

Between Budleigh itself and the Pebblebed cliff, you pass below desert dune sandstone (the Otter Sandstone) wind-eroded into sculptural curves. At the very foot of this a striking yellow band is a stony desert floor that the dunes blew across and covered. 'Dreikanter' (three-sider) pebbles are formed when wind-blown sand smooths down one side for centuries, until some chance turns the pebble over for another face to be scoured in it.

Fossil tree roots behind the beach huts at Budleigh Salterton

At the village end turn left on a path around a car park to the Otter Estuary. The path follows the edge of the wetlands, past a bird hide, to a lane. ▶ Cross the lane to the continuing riverside path. (Otter Sandstone is on the far bank, mixed dunes and flash flood deposits.) After 1.2km, the metal Clamour Bridge is seen ahead. Just before reaching it, bear left on a footpath that crosses a concrete flood weir, then curves left on a raised flood embankment. The path becomes enclosed, then joins a track on its left to run out to the corner of a lane.

Turn left, to the **B3178** at the Rolle Arms at the edge of East Budleigh. Cross into Lower Budleigh, which becomes Middle Street. ▶ Middle Street runs north, past the Drake School, to reverse the outward route to the car park on Hayes Lane.

If the wetland path is flooded, an alternative path runs north to the same lane. Continued to the east, the lane leads to a bridge over River Otter joining Walk 3

At this point, behind a large horse chestnut on the left, is an old barn The Pound built of Devon cob, a mix of straw and red mud.

WALK 3

Otterton, Peak Hill and the Otter

Start/Finish	The Green, Otterton SY 081 852
Distance	21km (13 miles); or shorter version 12km (7½ miles)
Ascent	400m (1400ft); or shorter version 250m (800ft)
Approx time	6hrs; or shorter version 3½hrs
Terrain	good paths, reasonably mud-free even in winter
Maps	Explorer 115 Exmouth; Landranger 192 Exeter & Sidmouth
Parking	street parking at The Green and at White Bridge (SY 074 830) on Otter estuary; on the longer route only, at Newton Poppleford and on Mutter's Moor (SY 109 872)

The Otter Sandstone is typical of the red desert rocks that form the Devon section of the Jurassic Coast (the bit of it that's actually in the underlying Triassic Period). Where better to appreciate them than along the River Otter itself? Well, actually the even-better bit is along the magnificent coast northwards from Danger Point, rising from the sea stacks of Ladram Bay to the twin peaks west of Sidmouth.

As well as enjoying six hours of cliff top and riverside, you get to examine the sand dune structures and the contrasting ones created by flash-flood seasonal rivers, and cross a hilltop of flinty, cherty Greensand.

GREENSAND
MERCIA Mudstn
OTTER Sandstone

The opposite riverbank shows the red Otter Sandstone, with layered stream-bed deposits and blank areas of sometime sand dune.

Head west out of the village to cross **River Otter** and turn left in a well-surfaced riverside path. Follow it downstream for the next 2.5km. ◄ Go past a footbridge end, and cross the side stream from an aqueduct arriving from the right. The good path continues along a raised causeway alongside the river, with fields to the right flooded in winter.

The path meets a lane. Turn left, signed Coast Path, on White Bridge across **River Otter** – parking area here. At the junction beyond turn right, and in 50 metres bear off right on a path along the right-hand edge of a field – the Otter estuary is behind trees on your right. At the

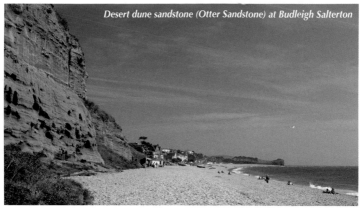

Desert dune sandstone (Otter Sandstone) at Budleigh Salterton

estuary mouth you can look across the Otter and along the shingle spit towards Budleigh Salterton. Turn left along a field edge, to arrive above south-east facing cliffs.

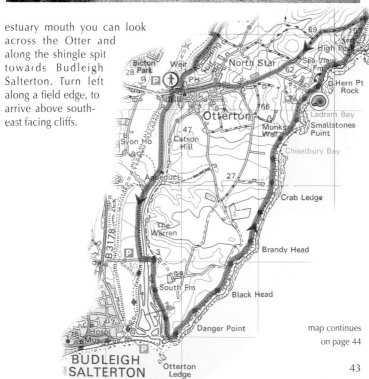

map continues
on page 44

43

A first look at the **Great Unconformity** (see 'Introduction') comes at High Peak, Peak Hill and along the coast eastwards. The red Triassic rocks are cut off at the top by the yellowish and much younger Greensand.

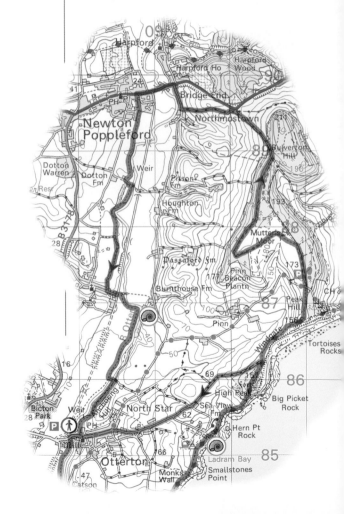

The grassy cliff top path after 1.5km reaches **Brandy Head**, a wartime observation point. Sea stacks are visible ahead and in another 1.5km you emerge to a field sloping down towards **Ladram Bay**. Here **Smallstones Point**, down to right of the path, gives clearer views of the bay. With a caravan settlement on your left, pass along a cliff top football pitch to its back left corner and a gate. Keep ahead past a track down right. ▸ Pass around to the right of Ladram Bay's restaurant bar complex to a gate into cliff top fields.

This track leads to the pebbly beach behind the sea stacks.

OTTER SANDSTONE

During the Triassic period (250 million years ago) the UK was a desert in the same climate zone as today's Sahara. A nearby mountain range supplied gravel in occasional flash floods down seasonal streams (wadis) to spread in great fans over the plains below. The finer sand blew away, to form desert dunes. All of this (and a bit more) can be seen in the Otter Sandstone.

The plainer areas are former dunes: at Ladram Bay you can see the slantwise pattern of overlying dunes ('cross-bedding'). In the cliff at Budleigh Salterton (Walk 2) is a desert floor that remained stable long enough to be oxidised yellow. Elsewhere are thin-layered stream-bed deposits: they also show diagonal cross-bedding on a smaller scale. Behind Budleigh Salterton's beach huts are the roots of desert bushes, outlined in calcite mineral (see Walk 2). The cliff above the River Otter (pictured), on the return leg of this walk, has it all: cross-bedded stream deposits, calcite tree roots, a purplish mud channel lens, and another fragment of yellowish desert floor.

On High Peak, heading inland

The slope steepens abruptly and is wooded as you cross up onto the Greensand cap of High Peak. At the wood top, the path becomes a wide track contouring around the inland face of **High Peak** (its southeast side has dropped into the sea). Up right, flinty ground has been planted with tree saplings. From the west of the summit, a steep path runs directly uphill, through an earthwork ring at the top, and up steps to the airy trig point.

Return to the track below and follow it on around the hill, dipping through a tree band to a signpost. ◀ Turn right for 100 metres to a bench with a view ahead to the grand cliffs of Peak Hill, their red Otter Sandstone topped off with yellowish Greensand.

On the short-cut route, you'll be returning to this signpost in a moment.

Short cut back to Otterton

If you've spent too long looking at Ladram Bay's rocks, or you want to spend the afternoon examining even more Otter Sandstone at Budleigh Salterton, then turn back at this point to Otterton, less than an hour away.

Return to the signpost just passed, and keep ahead, signed for Otterton. The hedged track (Bar's Lane) runs within the tree belt, then downhill to a road corner at

Seaview farm. Keep ahead along the tarmac Ladram Road, passing the entrance to Ladram Bay caravan site on your left. The lane runs down into **Otterton**, where you keep ahead at a junction into the main street, passing the Kings Arms to reach the Green at the walk start.

Beyond the bench the track diminishes to a path, turning down left through a kissing gate, then heading to the right along field tops alongside the cliff top. The path crosses the **Windgate** col to a gate. Here bear right on the path up next to the cliff top.

> The steep, gorsey ground lies on the **Greensand cap** of the hill; underfoot are flints. These are all that remain from the chalk that once lay above the Greensand. That chalk has been dissolved and washed away, leaving only its insoluble flints.

The path levels at an interpretation board. Continue across the top of **Peak Hill** to a signpost. Turn left for Mutter's Moor, inland, across grassland to the left of a hedge, to cross a road to a car park entrance. Keep ahead, to the right of the car park, into a track through woods. After 500 metres bear left on a waymarked path through scrubby gorse of **Mutter's Moor**. Join a wider path (arriving from the left) to a track junction.

Here turn left, following waymarks with blue (bridleway) arrows, soon bearing right on the main track. The flinty-surfaced track runs over open heath with scattered pines. At the corner of a pine plantation, join a better-surfaced track ahead (it arrives from down left). In another 200 metres the track bends right. ▶ The track runs along the top of steep slopes, with views to the left across the Otter Valley. Soon it runs under trees, then descends to a track junction in a col. Just up ahead is a metal bench marked as being Keble's View.

Bear left, on a track passing just below Keble's View bench and slanting down northwest, between hedges. At Four Elms (mobile phone mast) it meets a washed-out old road. Turn left down this. It becomes deeply sunken

A side track on the left now is a short cut to Colaton Raleigh.

between walls of red stone. Farm vehicles have got bigger, and if one comes up the lane you'll have to scramble up the high banking.

At the lane foot, meet a tarmac lane near **Northernmost Farm**. Turn right onto A3052, and then left over **River Otter** into **Newton Poppleford**. ◄

With the village centre uphill ahead, turn left (south) into Millmoor Lane. Keep ahead into a signposted narrow path out between houses into fields. The path follows the top of the bank above River Otter's flood plain, to a turning circle below **Dotton Farm**. Turn left to the riverbank. Don't cross the footbridge, but turn downstream to right of River Otter. The path heads into woods through a damp gateway, bending left above a river bend, and runs along the top edge of a narrow field.

Look out for a waymarked gate and kissing gate on the right – pass through and continue to right of the hedge. Pass a side path on the right, to enter a wide, hedged path. After 600 metres bear left down a track to meet a lane at the edge of **Colaton Raleigh**.

Turn left to **River Otter**. Again, don't cross the footbridge ahead but turn downstream along the river bank. Soon on the opposite bank is an ivy-draped showpiece of Otter Sandstone. After 1km you reach a high-arched footbridge, named Rickety Bridge, although currently firm and substantial. Cross it and turn right, on a field path above the river. After 800 metres it runs down to the Green in **Otterton**.

Walls and cobblestones here are of Budleigh Salterton pebbles – the village is named after the 'popples' or pebbles. There's a shop and pub, and takeaway food.

WALK 4

Sidmouth to Weston

Start/Finish	Sidmouth west end SY 120 871
Distance	14km (9 miles); or shorter version 12km (7½ miles)
Ascent	450m (1500ft); or shorter version 200m (700ft)
Approx time	4½hrs; or shorter version 3hrs
Terrain	grassy cliff top paths (some steep ascents and descents); tracks and paths, with tarmac driveway and paths after Knowle House
Maps	Explorer 115 Exmouth & Sidmouth; Landranger 192 Exeter & Sidmouth
Parking	Manor Road long-stay pay and display (car parks in the town centre are more expensive and miss the Otter Sandstone walkway)

With descents to sea level at Salcombe Mouth and (optionally) at Weston Mouth, plus Sidmouth itself, this combines quite strenuous cliff top walking with quite a lot of close-up rocks. While those rocks are mostly the featureless Mercia Mudstone, there's Otter Sandstone with its lively streams and sand dunes at Sidmouth, and fallen chunks of Greensand, perhaps with fine seashells, at Salcombe Mouth. Finally, the optional descent to Weston Mouth shows that mudstone isn't altogether dull...

The return walk is simply the quick way back to Sidmouth, through town parkland alongside River Sid.

On the seaward side of the car park descend steps to the main road (Peak Hill Road). Turn right for 50 metres, then left under a flint archway at the edge of Connaught Gardens. Pass along a terrace (Clock Tower Café is through an arch on your left) to descend the steep, white-painted cliff stairway Jacob's Ladder to the beach top. A walkway (not accessible during high tide storms) passes along below red cliffs. At its end, join the esplanade along the seafront.

CHALK
GREENSAND
MERCIA Mudstn
OTTER Sandstone

SIDMOUTH RED BEDS

Looking west from Jacob's Ladder, High Peak and Peak Hill are the start of the Great Unconformity, with yellowish Greensand peeping through the tree-covered tops. Below is soft, red Mercia Mudstone; but at the foot of High Peak, the more solid and patterned Otter Sandstone forms the sea stack Picket Rock and

Reduction bands including root traces, in Otter Sandstone at Jacob's Ladder

the lower cliff before sliding down to sea level. So here you can just about detect the 'angular unconformity', with the old, red, lower strata tilted relative to the Greensand on top.

A fault plane running through the back of Jacob's Ladder bay brings the Otter Sandstone back up from under the sea. The beach-top walkway gives a chance to look at its two sorts of bedding, the large-scale swirly sand dunes and the gritty, narrow-banded flash flood streams. The interpretation boards at each end of the walkway are helpful in recognising these features.

The red of the sand is iron oxide – basically, rust – although not originally this cheerful brick red. Just as bricks are fired in the kiln, the Red Bed was coloured by baking underground in the process of rock formation. But it's interleaved with bands of greenish-grey. Here some plant life has managed to get growing. Decomposing in stagnant pools, it has locked up all the oxygen and thus changed the colour. These are reduction bands, where 'reduction' is the chemists' term for de-rusting, the removal of oxygen. Grey-green squiggles down out of the bands were tree roots reaching into the red mud. The interpretation board also offers 'possible reptile burrows'. You may or may not be convinced by these...

At the eastern end of Sidmouth's esplanade, you can look across to where the Otter Sandstone with wide and striking grey-green reduction bands forms the foot of the cliff, giving way to the featureless Mercia Mudstone above.

Just in case anyone's disappointed not to see any of the **igneous rocks** – Devon Council has been helping out. Glistening grey-black blocks along the shoreline at Sidmouth have been specially imported from Norway to keep out the sea; but also to make a change from the sedimentary rocks – ones laid down on sea beds, lake beds or in deserts – which make up the whole of the Jurassic Coast.

These black, big-crystal magmas cooled slowly, in a huge magma chamber many miles under the ground. They come under the general family name of gabbro (misnamed by kitchen salesmen as 'black granite'). Away from Sidmouth and Lyme Regis sea defences, see gabbro in the Cuillin Hills of Skye, and in the counter top of every Ritazzo coffee stall.

At the end of the esplanade bear left to a footbridge on the right. Across it, head up a zigzag path then up the street (Cliff Road) above. After 200 metres, follow markers briefly left, then up right again. At the top of the lane

51

turn right to reach a cliff top field with buttercups. At the field top, with a bench, the ground steepens into a wood with bluebells in spring. Emerge to a brief level bit on **Salcombe Hill**. At a bench, the Coast Path reaches the top of a long, steep flight of steps, the toughest descent between Minehead and Poole.

Short cut by Salcombe Regis

Although you miss a fine bit of coastline, here you can bear down left, on a slanting grass path inland. This levels at a field gateway, and runs to the start of a gravel track above yellow South Combe Farm. The track runs out to the lane at the foot of **Salcombe Regis**. Turn up through the village, past the church (Greensand, with some fossil shells). At the T-junction at the Salcombe Regis Thorn turn right, and follow the lane for 800 metres to the main **A3052** road.

Head to the right on a bike path alongside the road for 50 metres, then cross to a gate with bridleway signpost. Go down with hedge on your left to a gate, and continue in the same line down a grassy dip to a gate at the field's bottom corner. Through this continue on a damp woodland track. After 400 metres, turn left over a stile with gate. Head down beside an electric fence, and at its corner turn right, through three small gates, to a signpost above bungalows and **Knowle House**. Turn down left, to a gate onto a tarmac lane above the houses.

Looking east to Weston Cliff from Higher Dunscombe Cliff

GREENSAND AT SALCOMBE MOUTH

The 'cliffs' at Salcombe Mouth are slopes of red Mercia Mudstone Clay. But 400 metres east of the beach path, large blocks of Greensand have tumbled from the cliff top, and this is a good place to see the natural stone in its freshly broken state. The broken surfaces can reveal fine fossil clams.

Green glauconite mineral in Greensand, seen at Hooken Beach

The Greensand is actually yellowish brown. But this colour is the result of weathering in the rain and oxygen of today's air. The chunks on the beach here do show the original greenish tinge of the mineral called glauconite. This forms in sluggish, organic-rich but oxygen-low sea beds, suggesting that the early Cretaceous sea was a stagnant and rather stinky one – the later formation of chalk on top of the Greensand marks what could be considered an even more unhealthy ecosystem.

Turn down right, and just through a massive hedge gap turn right again into a fenced-in path. This runs down to a bridleway T junction on the main route.

Head down the steep earth and wood steps, then down the right-hand edges of two more fields. At the bottom right corner is a signpost and kissing gate. The Coastal Path will turn left, inland, along the field foot above Salcombe Mouth stream valley. But first, take the path down through the kissing gate into scrub, then down steps to the shingle beach at **Salcombe Mouth**.

Return up to the kissing gate, and turn right, inland, along the rim of the stream hollow (or 'goyal') to cross a footbridge. ▶ Head diagonally up a field to the cliff top, then up the steeper wooded path in zigzags. At the level hilltop, continue along field edges next to the sea to a corner with bench and a view above Littlecombe Shoot.

Turn left here, contouring inland to a signpost. Turn right, across a wooded stream bed (dry), and ahead up

To the left of the stream is a path to Salcombe Regis.

steps to another signpost (ignoring a downhill path beside the stream). A wide grass path contours across the slope, below a large patch of flints gathered to make a sea marker.

The path continues through knolly ground and past Greensand cliffs; then it zigzags down through a wood. Ignore a signposted path towards Dunscombe but instead turn down right, to emerge at a field below the wood. At its bottom corner is a gate and signpost above for **Weston Mouth**. ◄

Here you could descend to the shore, with notes on Weston Mouth at the following Walk 5.

Turn inland, signposted for Dunscombe. A path runs alongside the tiny stream to a gateway. Now a rough track, it bears up left, away from the stream, to a grassland clearing at the wood top. Bear off right, signposted to the Donkey Sanctuary, on a path along the foot of the clearing, eventually with the stream again on your right. A fenced gravel path runs up to the **Donkey Sanctuary** at Slade House Farm. Pass through three gates to emerge at a road corner alongside the farm. Keep ahead up the lane to a T junction near the farm entrance. ◄

The Donkey Sanctuary is open daily until 5pm (4pm winter). Free entry.

Turn left past the farm entrance, then right in a dirt track. Keep ahead as it continues overgrown to the main **A3052**. Cross to the right to a bridleway sign, just above a gate marked 'Hurfords'. Head down the concrete track, then keep ahead in a fenced grass track between donkey fields into woodland. Follow an earth track around to the left. Ignore footpath arrows pointing down right as the track runs slightly uphill to a gate into open grassland.

Cross the slope ahead on an invisible path, with views to the right, contouring to another gate into woods. Here an earth track runs downhill. Fork down right to a gate onto a tarmac lane above houses at **Knowle House**. Turn down right, and just through a massive hedge gap turn right again, signposted, into a fenced-in path. This runs down to a bridleway T junction. ◄

The short cut route rejoins.

Turn left on a hedged bridleway path to join Knowle House's driveway. Turn right, and follow the tarmac drive out through a field then woodland to the edge of Steven's Cross. Cross into a housing estate, following Harcombe Lane as it bends left around the estate to reach **A3052**.

Turn right, to cross an ancient bridge into **Sidford**. At once turn off left into Ford Cottages. Opposite the Sidford Social Hall, take a gate on the left onto a tarmac bike/walker path. After 400 metres take a gate on the left into the meadows, following a grass path near the bike/walker one, and then rejoining it, except that it's now a gravel walkers' path (the bikes veered off). ▶

Soon you rejoin the tarmac bike/walker path, and then the River Sid. There's a footbridge here, which you can cross (or either of the two following ones) for a path along the Byes Riverside Park. It emerges into **Sidmouth** at a tollhouse cottage, with an ancient bridge (Willow Bridge) on your right. Don't cross that, but cross the road into Millford Road opposite.

Take the footbridge alongside a ford, and continue ahead in Mill Road to the first left, Riverside Road. You can fork off it to a riverside path, with Otter Sandstone dune and stream cross-bedding in the opposite riverbank. The path and road lead to the grey footbridge crossed earlier, and the eastern end of Sidmouth's esplanade.

Otter Sandstone with grey reduction bands, under featureless Mercia Mudstone, Sidmouth east end

Grassy meadows nearer the River Sid can also be followed.

WALK 5

Branscombe Mouth to Weston Mouth

Start/Finish	Branscombe Mouth SY 207 881
Distance	12km (7½ miles)
Ascent	350m (1200ft)
Approx time	4hrs
Terrain	paths and tracks, 1km of quiet lane; wooded valleys and cliff top fields
Maps	Explorer 115 Exmouth; Landranger 192 Exeter
Parking	pay and display at Branscombe Mouth

Weston Mouth's chert beach pebbles are awkward to walk on, especially when leaving the sea after a swim. But, along with the tall red mudstone rising behind, they give the place an atmosphere of its own. To examine the 'satin-spar' gypsum of the ancient lake beds, you'll pass through the nude-beach area. The easily embarrassed can get their gypsum at the walk's end at Branscombe, and blocks fallen from the cliff tops there give some of the best-preserved Greensand shells I've seen. The wooded valley descending to Weston Mouth contrasts with the bare chalk cliff tops of the return to Branscombe Mouth.

Weston Mouth and Salcombe Mouth (on Walk 4) are the quietest beaches on this section of the coast – understandably, given the mile of walk to reach them, with a steep final descent.

CHALK
GREENSAND
MERCIA Mudstn

Above the thatched café, at a 'coast path' signpost, turn right on a smooth gravel path; this runs inland to the left of a stream, then crosses it. The path up-valley runs into the end of a lane, which runs into **Branscombe**. Turn left over the stream to a small car park on the right, opposite the National Trust's Old Bakery café.

A gravel path runs above the lane, to rejoin it just before a school. Turn right, up the lane; then keep ahead, and level, where the main lane forks up left. The tarmac continues gently uphill for 600 metres. At a junction above **Hole House**, the lane turns down right; here keep ahead on a rough tarmac lane marked 'No Vehicles'.

Ignore a bridleway forking up left. The lane becomes

Track to Edge Barton above Branscombe

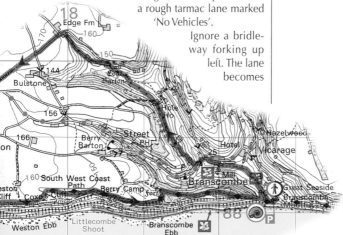

57

a rough track, level then down to the right to cross the stream. In a field with 'Beware of the Bull' threat (no bull when I passed), the track is soggy before slanting up to a gate, where it joins a tarmac driveway between houses.

Head up this lane to **Edge Farm**. The lane bends left across the chalk plateau, to a road, which you cross to a stile. A green path runs with hedges to its left, to a stile onto a track between high hedges. At a farm it becomes gravel track to a lane.

Turn right to a junction, where you keep ahead for Salcombe Regis. At the next junction, just before the main entrance to the **Donkey Sanctuary**, turn down left, signed for Stoneleigh Holiday Village.

Where the lane bends left, keep ahead on a gravel path to left of donkey pens through three successive gates. At the path foot, don't cross the stream on the left but head down the field edge beside it. Continue along the foot of a long, grassy clearing, now with trees below, on a path that meets a stony track. Bear left down this track to the stream, and follow it to a kissing gate with signpost in the field corner.

Grey reduction bands and pink gypsum crystals in red Mercia Mudstone, Hook Ebb by Weston Mouth

The valley ends abruptly above the sea: it's a **hanging valley**, its lower part now washed away. For its last 400 metres the stream drops in a deep wooded slot as it works its way down to the new sea level.

Bear left down the steep path to the shingle shore at **Weston Mouth**. (Back right (west) along the shingle for 800 metres is **Hook Ebb** with gypsum display.) Cross the

GYPSUM AT WESTON MOUTH AND BRANSCOMBE MOUTH

At Hook Ebb, 1km west of Weston Mouth, the red Mercia Mudstone rocks have streaks of pinkish-white. These are dried-up lake beds, such as in California's Death Valley today. The mineral is gypsum, as used in plasterboard – gypsum is light, cheap and has fire retardant qualities because of the water molecules incorporated in its crystals.

Gypsum crystals, Hook Ebb by Weston Mouth

In Death Valley the mineral is smooth and white, resembling concrete. Under the heat and pressure of rock formation, the gypsum at Weston Mouth has recrystallised into the 'satin spar' form, like the bristles of a toothbrush or a dry ski slope. The grey-green bands are 'reduction bands', see Walk 4.

Shells in Greensand, beach boulder at Branscombe Mouth

West from Branscombe Mouth, past beach huts, the red Mercia Mudstone again has strips of white gypsum mineral with satin spar crystals. The gypsum has been split and sliced by sideways movements in the rocks.

Here too are slabs of yellowish Greensand and white Beer Head limestone fallen from the cliff tops. Both the Greensand and the limestone have shelly fossils.

The field to your left is original chalk meadow with cowslips in spring, knapweed later.

stream (or walk around its foot as it vanishes into the shingle). At once take a steep path back up the hanging scrub to the corner of a field. Continue up this field, rejoining the cliff top edge, with the ascent steepening at the top. Along **Weston Cliff**, a thorny hedge conceals the sea. ◄

At a signposted gate, the coast path bears left to cross a dip to a field gate. Bear right, contouring along the meadow beyond to rejoin the cliff top. Pass through the low earthworks of **Berry Camp**, some of which has vanished over the cliff edge.

The path meets the end of a track, which you follow to the left for 150 metres to a T junction. Turn right along the top edge of a wood with Branscombe village down below. The track diminishes to a path, which rejoins the cliff tops to descend to **Branscombe Mouth** car park.

Upper Greensand blocks below Higher Dunscombe Cliff east of Salcombe Mouth: in the cliff itself chalk (at the very top), Upper Greensand, pale green Foxmould, red Mercia Mudstone

WALK 6
Beer and Hooken Undercliff

Start/Finish	Beer, above beach SY 229 891 or at Branscombe Mouth SY 207 881
Distance	6.5km (4 miles)
Ascent	300m (1000ft)
Approx time	2½hrs
Terrain	grassy cliff top; narrow, rough and sometimes slippery path in wooded undercliff
Maps	Explorer 115 Exmouth and 116 Lyme Regis (need both); Landranger 192 Exeter
Parking	pay and display in Dolphin Road, behind Dolphin Hotel; Cliff top car park SY 226 888 is less busy and a bit cheaper; pay and display at Branscombe Mouth

The place behind the landslip – the undercliff – is a world of its own. Below, you look down over cliff tops to the sea; above, you look up to more cliffs. The ground is lumpy and split by unexpected chasms. And the awkward, half-way-up patch of land is a naturally formed nature reserve, with bushy vegetation, butterflies and birds.

The Lyme Undercliff walk (Walk 8) plunges you into this wild (if rather narrow) world for a full day's walking. The Hooken Cliffs are the same thing at a convenient smaller scale.

From just above **Beer** beach, head up Common Road, a one-way street uphill, with its stepped terrace of flint houses. At a crossroads keep ahead, marked 'no through road'. The lane passes Clifftop long stay parking, then runs above Beer Head Caravan Site. Where the road bends right towards a farm, keep ahead past a map board onto a track across a cattle grid. It follows the top edge of a field, with a fence to its right.

At a gate bear right on a faint track, and pass to left of a tower house onto a wide, grassy cliff top path. As it

CHALK
GREENSAND
MERCIA Mudstn

Chalk cliffs at Beer

The walk could start and finish at the car park here; see also box on gypsum in Walk 5.

starts downhill (direct to Branscombe Mouth, but steep) bear right, through a gate with signpost. A faint path across the cliff top field becomes an earth track slanting down among trees. It bends back left, muddy sometimes and cow trodden. Turn down right through a gate, for a hedged path to Great Seaside house and the lane below. Turn left to **Branscombe Mouth** car park. ◄

At the road foot, turn up left through a gate. A wide grass path slants up the field. At its end, don't turn up the main path to cliff tops.

Instead keep forwards on a track through huts. At the end of the huts, the path leads forward into the undercliff. The path rambles up and down in dense scrubland, until a short side path could lead you down to the beach.

There's a fine view up to the Hooken Landslip **pinnacles**, eastwards along the beach. Greensand blocks on the beach are fresh enough to have traces of the green glauconite mineral that gives the rock its name. White, shelly rocks are the Beer Head Limestone.

BEER STONE AND BEER HEAD LIMESTONE

Chalk is pretty soft stuff. But a particular layer at Beer has a strange quality: it hardens as it dries out after being quarried. Before it hardens it's easy to carve; over half of England's cathedrals have interior work, like statues and carved screens, of Beer Stone. Its quarry caves, above the village, were worked for over 2000 years. They're now a home for hibernating bats in the winter and a tourist resort the rest of the time.

Beer Stone is not a normal chalk. A sea current washed away the powdery coccoliths, the skeletons of algal slime, and Beer Stone is mostly broken-up sea urchins.

Beer Head Limestone (or 'Cenomanian Limestone') isn't the same as Beer Stone, but is another untypical sort of chalk. It's the chalk's lowest layer, immediately above the yellower Greensand, and is often made up of broken seashells.

Past this junction, the main path rises gradually along the gap behind the chalk pinnacles that stand above the sea. Pass under an adit hole in the upper cliffs. ▶ The path rises along the undercliff valley and then up the grassy slope above. High on the upper cliff slope it zigzags back left to reach the cliff top just above, at a gate and signpost.

The landslip has exposed one of the old mines into the Beer Stone.

Turn right, past **Beer Head**, and along cliff top fields towards Beer. Opposite the caravan site the path turns left, inland. After a short rise turn right below the caravan site on a tarmac path which becomes Little Lane. At its end, turn right down Common Lane to its foot above the beach at **Beer**.

FOSSILISED SEA FLOOR

Hardground (fossil sea bed) with Beer Head Limestone above Greensand, beach boulder at Branscombe Mouth

Sand, or chalky sludge, sifts slowly down onto the sea bottom, eventually to form the thick slabs of Greensand or of chalk. But sometimes there's a pause, when the same sea floor endures for thousands of years. Chemical action is gradually hardening it, but at the same time it's being burrowed and reshaped by shrimps and worms. Then the sea currents readjust, the rock sludge drizzles down again, and the former sea floor is buried intact.

At the western end of Beer's beach you see at least three such fossil sea bottoms, or 'hardgrounds'. One is at the very base of the cliff, forming the top surface of the yellower Greensand. Two more are in the somewhat shelly Beer Head Limestone that forms the lowest metre of the white chalk above.

These sea floors are, of course, the right way up, with the burrow-scrambled rocks on the underside of the hardground. At Branscombe Mouth, chunks of the Beer Head Limestone layer have fallen onto the beach. You can use the hardgrounds to work out which of these chunks are upside down. Such 'way-up structures' can be important. It's a bad mistake to assume a rock formation is the right way up when it isn't.

WALK 7
Hartridge and Dumpdon

Start/Finish	Luppitt ST 169 068
Distance	Hartridge 7.5km (4½ miles); Dumpdon 1.5km (1 mile)
Ascent	Hartridge 250m (800ft); Dumpdon 50m (150ft)
Approx time	Hartridge 2¼hrs; Dumpdon 45mins
Terrain	paths, horrendously boggy for a short distance on Hense Moor, then firm and dry
Maps	Explorer 115 Sidmouth; Landranger 192 Exeter or 193 Taunton
Parking	Hartridge Luppitt Church; then tiny National Trust car park north of Dumpdon Hill
Note	the walk is in two sections with separate start points 3km (2 miles) apart – the drive takes 10mins; or it is a 1km walk through Beacon from the southern end of Hartridge but it is tricky walking along high-hedged lanes with blind corners

Southeast Devon has a simple two-layer structure. Above, the plateau of flat-lying Greensand. But where erosion has broken through that, the ground drops abruptly to the rounded valleys carved out of the softer Mercia Mudstone.

Luppitt's church, built from yellowish Greensand and the shiny chert lumps dotted within it, stands high up the valley side, on the firm Greensand bedrock. Many of the farms lie along the junction line, half way up the slope, where the rainwater reaches the waterproof mudstone, and emerges in a line of springs. The two rock layers are well hidden under the lively greenery of this lush farmland. But you are well aware of the transition anyway: as the path along Hense Moor dips below the spring line, your feet sink, and the mud trickles around your ankles...

Wet-and-dry sandpaper is more effective than either alone. Hense Moor's nature reserve has wet and dry heath, with twice as many rare orchids in a small space. But instructive as it is to experience that geological sogginess, a kilometre and a half of it is enough. Shake off the mud on the airy traverse along the Hartridge, with wide views across the top of the Otter. And as 3km aren't really enough of that, there's an add-on summit at Dumpdon Hill, a few kilometres to the south.

GREENSAND
MERCIA Mudstn

Luppitt Inn, attached to the end of a farm house, supposedly has an underground pipe direct to Otter Brewery at the north end of the walk.

A gate leads down to the church. Continue down the road towards **Luppitt** village (such as it is) and Luppitt Inn. ◀ Just above the pub turn left in a roughly tarred track with bridleway signpost. As it bends uphill, turn down sharp right (bridleway waymarker) on a rough earth track into open woods. Turn down through the wood to a lower track along its foot, and turn left, away from Luppitt, into the wet-and-dry nature reserve.

The track is muddy, but with a firm chert base. As the hedge on the right turns away, keep ahead, slightly uphill, on a faint path with some horrendous boggy bits as it follows the spring line at the base of the Greensand. There are a couple of waymark posts, before a stile where you cross a driveway to a small gate.

The path leads slightly uphill through woods – a groove below it may be the leat or ditch along the spring line to gather the water. In a few steps emerge suddenly onto dry grassland, keeping about 40 metres above a hedge and open field.

A waymark marks the path ahead, descending into soggy woodlands and turning down right to a footbridge. Continue north, with an earth bank on your right, to a concrete driveway with house ('dogs loose') just below. Take a few steps up the driveway, then turn up right through a field gate.

Continue above the earth bank at the foot of **Hense Moor** nature reserve, slanting uphill then level. When the bank turns down right, keep ahead, slanting

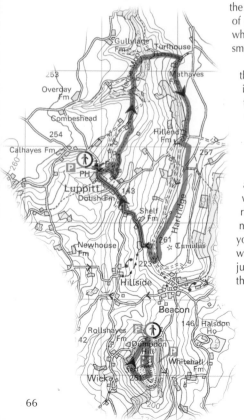

downhill below a phone wire to a gate, and a woodland path down to a footbridge. Keep ahead through a small swamp, and up to left of a stream to a driveway corner.

Take the tarmac track bearing up right, with the stream to its right. After a stiff climb, the lane bends left but turn right on a gravel track above **Malthayes Farm**. ▸ Keep ahead below the hedge at the top of the steep slope, with great views. The farm just below is also the Otter Brewery, smelt rather than seen.

Follow the slope top along the top edges of several fields (one of them has a fine pile of chert lumps collected off the fields). Keep ahead along a strip of grassland above woods. At the next gate, a waymarker points slightly down right. Slant down the field to a driveway above **Hillend Farm**, and exit to the corner of a lane.

Keep ahead for 50 metres, then turn left up a cleared path through bracken. Turn right on another cleared path along the slope top, to a lane. ▸

Cross slantwise, onto a path along the top of the steep **Hartridge** scarp, with a fence on its left. At the hill end, the path becomes a grass track, bending down left with views ahead to Dumpdon Hill.

Here the footpath has been diverted: you don't now drop to Malthayes Farm.

Alternative parking place here, ST 180 067.

On Hartridge, looking south towards Luppitt

At a track junction, turn down sharp right to the lane below. Turn left for a few steps, for the lane turning back down to the right. The lane is narrow and hedged, but traffic is light and locals also walk these lanes. At Barnfield Farm turn right, and follow the lane across a ford/culvert (dry unless the stream is very full, in which case there's a footbridge). The lane leads up past the Luppitt Inn to the church.

> **Luppitt church** is chert, with Greensand around windows and at corners. Inside, a spectacular Norman font shows hunting and martyrdom scenes and the weird beast, the amphisbaena – or, in the Dr Dolittle books, the Pushmi-pullyu – a hopefully non-existent beast capable of going in both directions at the same time.

Norman font with amphisbaena, Luppitt church

On Dumpdon Hill with Hartridge behind

Dumpdon Hill

A woodland path from the corner of the car park contours southwest. At the wood edge, turn up left on steep grassland. At the slope top, continue ahead (south) across a level field to the bracken-and-bramble covered earthwork and **Dumpdon Hill's** trig point at its centre.

Bear right (southwest) past the corner of the summit wood, and down a steep, rough path to a disconnected gate at the foot of the open slope. A fence and scrubland are just below. Turn right on a grass path around the base of the steeper slope, to the kissing gate on the outward route. Pass back through the wood to the small **car park**.

RED BED ROUNDABOUT

High Peak and Peak Hill

The Red Bed Roundabout from Newton Poppleford is a grand traverse across all of the Pebblebed Heaths – including the one at Mutter's Moor that's actually chert and flint lying on Greensand. This sets you up for a big chunk of the coast, from Budleigh's West Beacon Down to Ladram Bay, High Peak and Peak Hill. The distance is 33km (20½ miles) with about 850m (2800ft) of ascent – about 10hrs.

From Newton Poppleford car park (free), follow a stream to **Burrow**, and join the East Devon Way over heathland of **Harpford Common** onto **Colaton Raleigh Common**. Here you join Walk 1 above the MoD firing range, and follow it by **Woodbury Castle** and the **Floors cliff top** to pass along the seafront at **Budleigh Salterton**.

At the bridge over **River Otter**, there's a short cut home up River Otter (Walk 3 in reverse), which leaves out half of the coastal walking, but saves 2hrs if running out of time at the end of the day. Otherwise, switch to Walk 3 by **Ladram Bay** and **High Peak**, to return to **Newton Poppleford**.

2 THE LIAS

- Landslips of the Undercliff
- Layers of the Lias
- Ammonites at Lyme Regis
- Golden Cap
- More ammonites at Seatown
- Sea cliffs of Bridport

Bridport Sandstone at East Cliff (Walk 13)

INTRODUCTION

Around 200 million years ago, the shifting of the continents brought Great Britain to the shoreline of a newly forming ocean. A warm, shallow sea covered Dorset. That sea was full of life: shells and ammonites falling as fossils to the sea floor, or recycling limestone to form cement for the Jurassic rocks.

Near the shore, the sea bed is sand, or river pebbles; the rock it ends up as will be sandstone. Further out, only a thin mud drifts out from the land; the rock ends up as siltstone or clay. Still further out, neither sand nor mud but only dead sea creatures fall to the sea floor, bound together with the white mineral called calcite; the resulting rock is limestone. As the sea level falls or rises, the rock will switch from limestone to clay and back again.

During the lower part of the Jurassic, the sea bed switches from clay to limestone almost like the ticking of a clock. At Devonshire Cliff at Lyme Regis, there are more than 20 of these alternations; they're seen again in the hard and soft layers in Bridport's yellow cliffs.

In August 1914, a mathematician called Milutin Milancovitch was flung into prison by the Austrians for being a Serb in the wrong place. Happily, he

Heading up the west side of Golden Cap (Walk 10)

Golden Cap and Thorncombe Beacon from Eype Mouth (Walk 12)

had his fountain pen and some clean sheets of paper; and he saw World War One not just as a Europe-wide disaster, but also as his opportunity to work out certain rhythmic variations in sunlight caused by the Earth's orientation in space

The second of the Milancovitch cycles is caused by the way the Earth's axis wobbles over a timespan of 41,000 years. When the Earth is more tilted, winters are colder and summers are more summery. It's this slight tweak that seems to have caused the 'clockwork ocean', switching abruptly from a limestone to a clay state and back again.

The resulting stripy rocks are called the Lias, a Dorset miners' way of saying 'layers'. It reappears in Somerset and Glamorgan on either side of the Bristol Channel, lies under the English Midlands, and forms layered cliff faces again at Staithes on the coast of Yorkshire.

WALK 8
Lyme Regis Undercliff

Start	Axmouth Bridge SY 253 900
Finish	Lyme Regis, the Cobb SY 340 914
Distance	10.5km (6½ miles)
Ascent	at least 300m (1000ft)
Approx time	4hrs
Terrain	rough, muddy path with lots of climbing and descending through dense woods
Maps	Explorer 116 Lyme Regis; Landranger 193 Taunton
Parking	Holmbush car park, Lyme Regis SY 338 920
Note	buses from the Square or Holmbush car park in Lyme Regis to Seaton (X51, X53, 9A – roughly hourly)

The walk through the Undercliff is a classic challenge, well worth the hassle of the initial bus trip. The going is rugged and undulating, especially when it's muddy. There are no escape routes to the cliff top, nor any access to the shoreline below. It has something of the feel of a walk in America's Appalachians; no other woodland walk in England has this level of remoteness and commitment.

The woods are full of birdlife, with glimpses of the broken chalk and Greensand overhead. Otherwise, you can put away the geology guide until you get to the far end. Once at Lyme Regis, supposing you've any daylight left, there are grey-on-grey Lias stripes and fine big ammonites of Monmouth Beach, one of England's prime fossil spots.

CHALK
GREENSAND
BLUE LIAS
PENARTH Group
MERCIA Mudstn

Cross the **River Axe** on the old bridge alongside the road bridge, the latter built in 1877 and the oldest concrete bridge still in use. On rejoining the main road's pavement, turn right up a tarred driveway to the car park of a golf course. Keep ahead on a short track onto the golf course, and then on a faint grass path, marked with concrete ammonites inset into the grass, straight up through the golf course to enter a hedged track. At the highest point of this, turn right into a hedged path, emerging into a field.

WALK 8 – LYME REGIS UNDERCLIFF

Keep ahead along the left edge of the first field beside the hedge, and from its corner bear left to cross the next one diagonally on a green track. Bear left along the field's far side, with scrubby ground on your right (**Haven Cliff**) dropping to the sea.

The path slants down into the scrub, and after crossing Goat Island (see box) will remain within this wooded

---

BINDON LANDSLIP

At Bindon Cliff on Christmas Night in 1839, after an extremely wet autumn, a chunk of land just over a kilometre wide broke away and slid down towards the sea. A brand new chasm, 30 metres deep and 75 metres wide, formed behind it: meanwhile, at its foot, a long strip of sea bed rose into the air to form a narrow island stinking of dead seaweed.

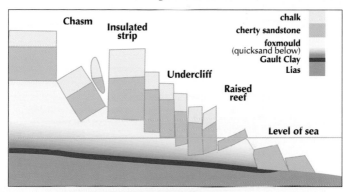

Bindon Landslip: diagram after William Dawson 1840. The Chert Beds and the Foxmould together constitute the Upper Greensand. The Foxmould is a foxy-coloured unconsolidated sand: the heavy rains of 1839 turned its lower part into a soggy slurry. ('Insulated' means turned into an island.) Geologists Conybeare and Buckland were on the spot within days, or possibly hours – they only had to come from Axminster. The only addition to their analysis here is the all-important Gault Clay.

Victorian lovers of romantic landscape were thrilled by this home-grown natural disaster. In Conybeare's words: *in grandeur of the disturbances it has occasioned, it far exceeds the ravages of earthquakes of Calabria and almost rivals the vast volcanic fissures ... on the flanks of Aetna.* The Navy planned a harbour behind the smelly island – at least until it washed away a couple of months later. Two fields of wheat and one of turnips, sown before the disaster, emerged on the broken off chunk of land, still known as 'Goat Island' (although not in fact an island).

But most excited of all were the geologists. Already they were speculating about what convulsion of the earth might have wiped out the great sea-monsters whose bones they'd been uncovering at Lyme Regis. Now here was their very own cataclysm, right on their Devon doorstep. The reason this 10km of coast keeps slipping so picturesquely into the sea is a slight seaward tilt of the strata. Water percolates through the chalk, and below it through the Upper Greensand, which here takes the form of a loose, foxy-coloured sand called the Foxmould. At the foot of the Foxmould it builds up against the Gault clay. Eventually, that clay forms a slippery layer for a chunk of chalk to slide gently down towards the waves. New fissures open every year, and now and then the Undercliff path gets closed because various bits of it no longer connect together.

undercliff for 6km to the edge of Lyme Regis. Note that throughout this length there will be no legal access to either the beaches below or the cliff top level above.

Cliffs above are mostly of chalk; rock at path level is a jumble of chalk and Greensand.

After crossing Goat 'Island', the narrow path, enclosed within high scrub or under trees, has only the rarest views of either the sea below or the cliffs above it. ◄ Occasional interpretation boards tell you how far along you've come.

After 3.5km the path joins a wider track. Turn right along this: a path down right for the shore

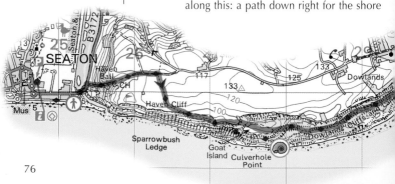

has warning notices and is not a right of way. After just 100 metres along the track, the coast path bears off to the right. In another 1km, at a junction with an interpretation board and some ruins, is a short path on the right to a sea view. The path then descends, and at another interpretation board becomes

Blue Lias at Monmouth Beach, Lyme Regis

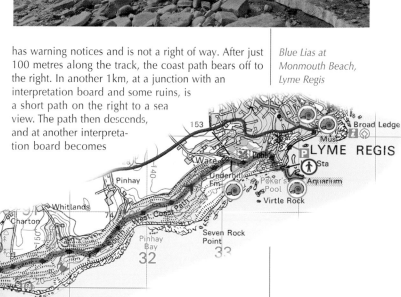

The Cobb, Lyme Regis

THE COBB

You look across the harbour to the town; and on its right, Black Ven, a laid-back slope of mudslides in grey clay and crumbly ochre sandstone. Jane Austen called it 'a very beautiful line of cliffs stretching out to the east of the town'. Perhaps the early Romantic sensibility was attuned to multicoloured mud. Whatever their aesthetics, however, these grey clays are great for ammonites (see Walk 9). The Austen quote is from *Persuasion*, largely set in Lyme and indeed on the Cobb itself.

Away to the right, the golden cap of Golden Cap and its neighbour Stonebarrow indicate that the Greensand layer of the Great Unconformity is still stretching eastwards. The sludgy Cretaceous sea-bottom, which away in the west cut off the tops of Permian Red Beds, is now lying on much younger Jurassic rocks. While the shadowly shape of the Portland Limestone appears dimly in the east.

But if, as you stand on the Cobb, a squall obscures the Isle of Portland – simply look down at your toes. The off-white stone underfoot is full of curly gastropod fossils. These are the 'Portland Screw'; the jetty has been repaired with Portland's Roach stone.

And if you still haven't seen enough sorts of stone – the black blocks dropped into the sea to protect the ancient jetty are crystalline volcanic rocks from Norway (gabbro, see Walk 4).

a disused tarmac road with cracks from ground subsidence.

After 600 metres the coast path forks off this old roadway, and in another 1km joins a slightly wider path arriving from back on the left. In another couple of hundred metres you emerge at a bend of the driveway of **Underhill Farm**.

Keep ahead along the driveway for 300 metres to a bungalow. Here fork off right on a field path. After a kissing gate into woods, take the right fork (signed for a viewpoint above the Cobb), soon with views over the sea. At the next path junction fork right for the Cobb, keeping right to a kissing gate at the top of woods. The path down through the woods leads by steps into the car park, just west of the Cobb.

MONMOUTH BEACH

Just 500 metres west of the Cobb, Monmouth Beach is the best quick ammonite excursion. Sea-washed limestone slabs have the outlines of dozens of large ones. Loose pebbles among the boulders have broken bits and pieces, refreshed by the sea twice daily; I found the corner of a fossil fish here.

At the back of the beach, the cliff is Blue Lias, actually grey-on-grey, showing the repeated layering of the Lias (see the introduction to this section). The upper part is fuzzier-looking Shales With Beef.

Large ammonite

WALK 9

Lyme Regis to Charmouth

Start/Finish	Holmbush Car Park, Lyme Regis SY 338 920 or Charmouth SY 364 931
Distance	9.5km (6 miles)
Ascent	250m (800ft)
Approx time	3hrs
Terrain	Field and woodland paths, pavements; shingle and boulder beach
Maps	Explorer 116 Lyme Regis; Landranger 193 Taunton
Parking	Avoid seafront. Pay and display at Holmbush Car Park on A3052 (Pound St) above the Cobb; during summer holiday period, park and ride from A3052 on both edges of the town. Parking at Charmouth closes 6.00pm
Note	Tidal beach. Leave Charmouth at least 3hrs before high tide for easy access below sea defences at Church Cliff. Once new defences east of Lyme are completed, there will be access along the top of them, so fewer tidal constraints. But tide half out or lower gives better choice underfoot and more ammonites.

The serious geologist will want no more than the walks Mary Anning and Elizabeth Philpot took almost every day: west to Devonshire Head and eastwards under Black Ven to Charmouth. But for those who want scenery as well as seashells, the route over Lyme Regis golf course gives you the Dragon's Hill and its views over the town, as a lead-in to some serious fossil-spotting along the beach from Charmouth. (The natural short route along the top of Black Ven has been 'temporarily' closed for many years due to landslips.)

Timing is the trick, as you want to leave Charmouth when the tide is falling or low. When low tides are in the morning, you could start in the walk from Charmouth.

MARY ANNING AND ELIZABETH PHILPOT

One day around 1810 a local carpenter's daughter sold an ammonite she'd found to a lady on the beach for two shillings and sixpence. At around £10 in today's money this was a useful cash supplement for a poor, working-class family – and as she grew up, Mary Anning

Cast of Mary Anning's first ichthyosaur, at Dorset County Museum, Dorchester

became the greatest fossil-hunter of her time: possibly of all time. At the age of 12 she dug out from the Lias of Lime Regis a 5m monster, inexplicable by the science of the time, and sold it for £23 – enough to feed her family for 6 months. It was the world's first plesiosaur.

The work was well-paid, but also dangerous. Her best finds were in winter, when the cliffs are at their most unstable. In 1833 she lost her pet dog and almost her own life in a rockfall. Eleven years later, she found the first ichthyosaur and sold it for a small fortune of £210. Later in life, she also found England's first pterodactyl.

Back in the 1820s, in class-ridden England, natural history did offer a hint of social mobility. Mary was respected by many of the gentlemanly geologists of her age, and friends with some of them. Her greatest discoveries are preserved in the Natural History Museum in London; a small museum in Lyme Regis is devoted to her life.

As a genteel unmarried lady, Miss Elizabeth Philpot had if anything even fewer opportunities in life than working-class Mary. Despite the social difference the two became close friends and collaborators, with Miss Philpot building an unrivalled knowledge of Lyme's fossil fish. The greatest palaeontologist of the time, Louis Agassiz, named two species of fossil fish for Mary Anning and one more for her friend.

Finding giant reptiles, or even fish, takes skill and persistence. There's just two places for the casual summer visitor to discover them: the Lyme Regis Museum, originally the Philpot Museum and based on Elizabeth's collection, and occupying Mary Anning's former fossil shop – or the 10,000 specimens in the free-enterprise Dinosaurland.

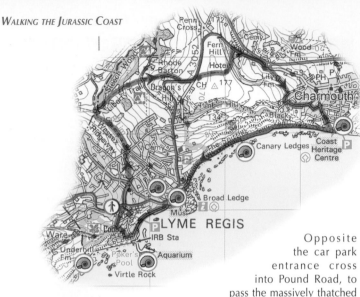

GREENSAND
Charmouth Mdstn
BLUE LIAS

Opposite the car park entrance cross into Pound Road, to pass the massively thatched Kersbrook Hotel. At the next junction cross slightly left into narrow Woodhead Road. After 25 metres, take a gate on the left for a path slanting down in woodland. It leads to a gate onto Roman Road, where you turn right, cross **River Lim** via Horne Bridge, and at once turn left in a small lane.

After passing a first footbridge (don't cross this one), keep ahead in the streamside path, to right of the stream then across a footbridge to enter a field. Keep upstream to another gate on the right, where you cross two footbridges to a large path with a thatched house over on your left.

Turn right, away from the thatched house, up the wide path signed for Dragon's Hill. It emerges into a field, and goes straight up the middle of it, and of another one above, to its top left corner, high on the flank of **Dragon's Hill**. Here emerge through a gate to the corner of a tarmac lane.

Head straight up ahead to the **A3052**. Cross onto a pavement, following it left to a junction in 200 metres. A path runs to right of the A road. After 100 metres, turn right, on a faint path across the golf course, following white paint marks on stones and trees. A gap leads into

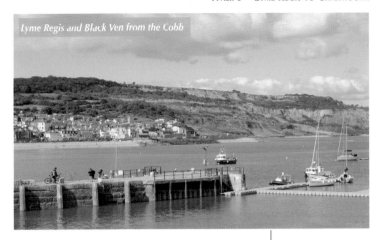
Lyme Regis and Black Ven from the Cobb

a wood. ▶ The path slants down leftwards to a gap onto the A3052.

Turn right, down the pavement past Fernhill Hotel (holisitic therapy, crazy golf and cream teas – everyone needs at least one of the three) to a major roundabout below. Pass round it to the first exit on the right, for Charmouth. In 50 metres at a footpath signpost turn up steps on the right. Just above, a rough track leads left into a field. Cross it slightly uphill, to pass between farm buildings made of chert. The farm's access track leads along a field top to a street at the top of **Charmouth**.

Turn right up the street, immediately bearing left on a lane that drops to another street. (Down ahead is another closed part of the Coast Path, but if reopened, use it!) Turn left, and at once right down Westcliff Road. At its foot, keep ahead to reach a descending street (Higher Sea Lane).

Where the street divides at its foot, keep ahead on an enclosed path signposted to the beach. This leads down to the car park at Charmouth Beach.

The Heritage Centre (upstairs) at **Charmouth Beach** is well worth visiting, with helpful staff who'll identify your finds. If desperate, there's a fossil shop

You're on the Greensand, and there are lumps of yellowish, flinty chert in the wood.

83

Black Ven

downstairs. For an easy (if inauthentic) fossil, the grey sea defences below the Heritage Centre show fine rugose coral – this is wrong by about 100 million years, as the boulders are Carboniferous Limestone imported from the Mendips.

Follow the foreshore (see note on tides in the information box above) under the grey mud cliff of **Black Ven**. The going is mostly coarse sand and shingle, with at least one short passage over boulders.

Pass below the grey-striped Lias cliffs of Church Cliff to the end of concrete sea defences at the edge of **Lyme Regis**. Steps lead up onto these, but the limestone slabs below have large ammonites on their top surface. Then ascend onto the concrete walkway below 'fortifications' (actually disguised sewage works). Cross a stream bridge below the Museum. Keep ahead along the esplanade (ammonite lamp standards) to **the Cobb**. ◄

See box, Walk 8.

Continue past the Cobb through the harbour car park, to turn inland and take a path to the left of a bowling green, then up steps between wooden huts. It crosses a road and continues up steep woodland beside a stream to a gate at the wood top. Through this turn right to

another gate. It leads to a tarmac lane (Pine Walk) past villas to the corner of the car park.

BLACK VEN

The 'cliff' is actually a pile of grey clay: mudslides are not uncommon, particularly in winter. Above is yellow Greensand, the bed of the Cretaceous sea (see 'Great Unconformity' in the Introduction).

Ammonites are pretty common here and you'd be unlucky to walk to Lyme Regis without spotting some. Look at

Ammonites on the beach, below Black Ven

pale grey sea-washed rocks too large for collectors to carry away; also inside flaking rocks of dark grey mudstone. With more time, sift through pebbles recently turned over by the sea. Belemnites (like lengths of grey pencil) are also found, and very occasional saurian vertebrae (backbone segments). Plesiosaurs and ichthyosaurs have been found here, but not by the casual visitor.

GOLDEN CAP

Stonebarrow and Golden Cap from below Black Ven

Golden Cap is celebrated as the highest point on England's south coast (time it for low tide to spot the remnants of past landslips below). The Anchor Inn at Seatown is celebrated as one of that coastline's nicest pubs (check out the seafood on the specials board). And Seatown's shingle beach is fairly good fossil country (with, for the sharp-eyed, a sign of England's worst-ever tsunami or tidal wave).

The short version (Walk 11) heads straight from the Langdon Hill car park to Golden Cap. The full Walk 10 sets off inland onto the Greensand heathland of Hardown Hill, in a triangle which then adds the fine 3km stretch of clifftop from Stonebarrow.

WALK 10
Hardown Hill, Golden Cap and Seatown

Start/Finish	Langdon Hill, west of Chideock SY 412 930 or Stonebarrow Hill SY 390 934
Distance	12km (7½ miles); or shorter version 10km (6 miles)
Ascent	550m (1800ft); or shorter version 400m (1300ft)
Approx time	4hrs; or shorter version 3¼hrs
Terrain	paths and tracks; heathy hill and grassy cliff tops
Maps	Explorer 116 Lyme Regis; Landranger 193 Taunton
Parking	at east end of dual carriageway section on A35, at top of the hill down to Chideock, an unsigned lane turns off to the NT car park on Langdon Hill; or car park at Seatown 9.30am–9.00pm

Golden Cap is a great viewpoint, but this walk adds in other good things beforehand. Hardown Hill has wide views inland, and a puzzle: can all this heather really be growing on chalky soil? The grassy clifftops at Stonebarrow are as good as any along this coastline. And the recently restored staircase down to St Gabriel's Mouth offers a really quiet beach and some less picked-over fossil terrain.

It'd be a great shame to linger too long at St Gabriel's and miss out on the full walk, not to mention tea at Seatown. But for such unfortunates, there is a short cut from Golden Cap straight back to the car park.

Take the track back down from the car park, and keep ahead along the roughly tarred lane you drove in along. At the T junction, keep ahead through a gate into fields. After two fields, cross the top edge of a third down to a gate at its corner. A nettly path leads round left to a track among houses. Turn up this, slanting up left to reach A35 in **Morecombelake** beside Moore's Biscuit Factory.

Cross A35 (pelican crossing just to left) and turn right for a few steps, forking left up Sun Lane. At its top it joins another lane. A few steps up this, turn left up a

GREENSAND

upper Lias

Charmouth Mdstn

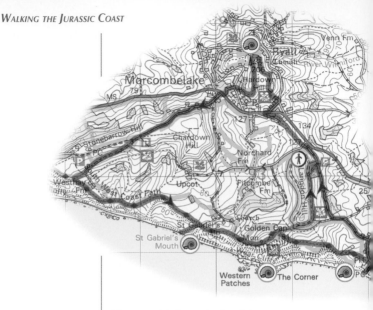

driveway with footpath sign. It becomes an overgrown, wooded path.

At the top of the wood continue through bracken for a few steps to the rim of **Hardown Hill**. Here turn right on a smaller path. This follows the rim of the hill, not far above the top edge of the wood you came up through. There are wide views on the right.

Keep following the small path around the hill rim. Soon there's heather on your left across the flat hilltop, and a radio mast. The path bears slightly left across the plateau, and meets a flinty track to the north of the radio mast.

We are on part of the former **Greensand plateau**, the bed of the Cretaceous sea that cuts across the top of all the older strata of Dorset. The observant will have seen the flints in the track, suggestive of chalk: but heather all around, and chalk is what heather simply refuses to grow on. Meanwhile those with noses in the map will have noted some matching heights: Hardown at 207m almost level

with Golden Cap at 191m, Chardown Hill at 194m, and Langdon Hill not much lower at 177m.

The matching heights are part of what was originally the flat plateau (and before that, a flat sea bed). Greensand is tougher than the underlying grey clays, so that at its edges the ground drops away steeply. And the flints? They came out of the chalk that once lay on top of the Greensand but has completely dissolved away in the rain, leaving land where heather is happy to grow.

Turn left, passing to left of the mast. Pass over the flat hilltop, and down past a plantation with a bench on your left. As the slope steepens, the track bends right and slants downhill, deeply sunken. It reaches a lane junction at the top of Morcombelake. Take the street down ahead to the **A35**.

Cross to the right, to enter Ship Knapp. The tarred lane runs uphill, then contours across the north slope of **Chardown Hill**. ▶ At the driveway of Grandview Farm bear left to a gate onto a rough track with bridleway signs. This has views across River Char vale. The track runs gently down to a gravel car park. ▶

Cross diagonally onto a stony track slanting downhill, signed for Westhay Farm. It has patches of tarmac,

On Hardown Hill, with Langdon Hill and Golden Cap behind

At Brackendene, a hedged path up left could take you on an alternative route over the top of Chardown Hill.

The walk could start and finish from the car park here.

89

between high hedges. Where the track bends down left (towards Westhay Farm) keep ahead, signed as Smugglers Path. The path can be overgrown and brambly. After 300 metres at a Coastal Path (and Golden Cap) signpost turn down left through a gate.

The path runs down through a meadow, with cliffs down to the right. Now it's just a matter of following the well-marked Coastal Path along the cliff tops towards Golden Cap, which rises ahead. Approaching the base of Golden Cap, the path drops towards a stream. Just before this, a gap stile on the right is the permissive path down to **St Gabriel's Mouth**. The path, restored in 2014, runs down through scrub, to reach the top of a steep wooden staircase down the grey clay to the shingle beach. About 200 metres left are fallen Greensand blocks on the beach – fresh enough to show green colour inside as well as fawn yellow.

Return up the ladder and scrub path to the open field above, and turn right, for the climb up Golden Cap. At the Greensand/grey clay boundary, the ground steepens abruptly and becomes scrubby with bracken and heather as the path zigzags to the summit of **Golden Cap**.

Golden Cap from the west

GOLDEN CAP: BOULDER ARCS

After a cliff landslide, the sea starts carrying away the mud and sand straight away. From the cliff top, you'll see the staining in the seawater: Permian pink, Jurassic grey or brown, Cretaceous chalky white. Pebbles will be transported away by the process of longshore drift (see Walk 16). Such erosion of the landslip's toe helps to gauge how long ago it happened.

The very biggest boulders in the landslip stay in place for thousands of years. Look down from near the trig point on Golden Cap at low-to-middling tide, and you'll see the boulder arcs that are the remains of former landslips from a time when the highpoint of the south coast was slightly higher, and 20 metres or so further south.

A Portland Stone memorial is on the left (with a corner of an ammonite on its back), before you reach the trig point. Bear down left to find a path with rope handrail to a kissing gate.

Head down cliff top fields to a gate into scrubby ground. A grass and mud path leads downhill, then through a small wood. Work around the foot of a large field to another small gate, with an enclosed path leading out to the lane just above **Seatown**. Turn down right to the Anchor Inn for bar and beach.

Return up the lane towards Chideock, past the foot of the path from Golden Cap, and keep uphill until a tarmac lane turns up left for Seahill House. After passing below the house the track becomes stony and hedged-in with no views. Head up it to a signpost. Here bridleways are marked ahead and backwards, but turn off right on a contouring track, passing above a wood. It then rises gently to a junction, where the stony wide track leads back up left to the car park on **Langdon Hill**.

Short cut via Langdon Hill

If time is short, from the kissing gate you could return directly to Langdon Hill car park. Keep straight down over a stile and across a grassy col to the woods at the base of Langdon Hill. Head straight up through them to a stony track, which contours to the right, around the hill, to the car park.

WALK 11
Golden Cap and Seatown

Start/Finish	Langdon Hill, west of Chideock SY 412 930
Distance	5km (3 miles)
Ascent	200m (650ft)
Approx time	2hrs
Terrain	paths and grassy cliff tops
Maps	Explorer 116 Lyme Regis; Landranger 193 Taunton
Parking	see

Sea views at Golden Cap, and seafood at Seatown's Anchor Inn. Enough said: who wants the tiresome 12km of Walk 10? There is, it's true, a stiff climb back from the beach to the car park on Langdon Hill – so send the driver up on his own and make him bring the car down to the sea.

GREENSAND
upper Lias
Charmouth Mdstn

From the end of the car park, pass through a gate with gap alongside it onto a wide path contouring south around the hill. You're on the Greensand, and the path is made of cherty lumps. In 800 metres the track bends west, and soon there's a bench with a view across to Golden Cap.

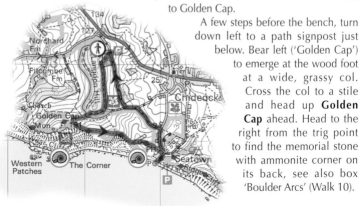

A few steps before the bench, turn down left to a path signpost just below. Bear left ('Golden Cap') to emerge at the wood foot at a wide, grassy col. Cross the col to a stile and head up **Golden Cap** ahead. Head to the right from the trig point to find the memorial stone with ammonite corner on its back, see also box 'Boulder Arcs' (Walk 10).

From Golden Cap's trig point, return down the path with rope handrail to the kissing gate, as used on the upward walk. ▶ Head down cliff top fields to a gate into scrubby ground. A grass and mud path leads downhill, then through a small wood. Work around the foot of a large field to another small gate, with an enclosed path leading out to the lane just above **Seatown**. Turn down right to the Anchor Inn for bar and beach.

If walking the full circuit of Walk 10, continue the route from this point.

TSUNAMI OF 1755

On a sunny afternoon on the terrace of the Anchor Inn, the sunlight picks out a horizontal line in the shingle bank on the far side of the stream, just below the foot of the car park. This is a narrow band of larger pebbles, and is interpreted as the deposit left by the tsunami that hit the south coast after the Lisbon earthquake on 1 November 1755.

Lisbon tsunami deposit, Seatown

The quake was a shifting on the Africa-Europe fault that runs through Gibraltar. It brought down the roof of Lisbon Cathedral during High Mass on one of the year's main religious festivals, All Saint's Day. Meanwhile those who'd skived off to the Alfama escaped largely unharmed – Alfama was the red light district. This threw into doubt the theory of such catastrophes as caused by sin, and liberated minds for alternative theories, the European Enlightenment, and the science of geology.

The tsunami wave on the English south coast is estimated at 3m (10ft), still large enough to cause flooding and many deaths in Cornwall. It is the UK's worst tsunami in historic times – although it's worth noting that 8000 years ago, during the Stone Age, a massive under-sea landslide off Norway sent a 20m tsunami, which washed 50 miles inland over the east coast of Scotland. Some of its deposits now form golf courses at St Andrews.

Meanwhile, on a still day on Loch Ness, the Lisbon Earthquake sent shock waves along the 22-mile loch, so that sudden waves broke on the shoreline at Fort Augustus. This caused residents to recall the legendary monster tamed by St Columba and to realise that Nessie was still down there somewhere.

A much earlier disaster has been detected at Seatown. High in the grey clays of Golden Cap, a tsunami or storm surge in the Jurassic sea of 190 million years ago suddenly buried creatures called brittle stars to form the Starfish Bed. Normally, these delicate creatures would decompose or get eaten up.

Seatown's Anchor Inn to Golden Cap

Return up the lane towards Chideock, past the foot of the path from Golden Cap, and keep uphill until a tarmac lane turns up left for Seahill House.

After passing below the house the track becomes stony and hedged-in with no views. Head up it to a signpost. Here bridleways are marked ahead and backwards, but turn off right on a contouring track, passing above a wood. It then rises gently to a junction, where the stony wide track leads back up left to the car park on **Langdon Hill**.

SEATOWN SUMMARY

Seatown's shingle is only moderately comfortable for sunbathing. But it's an excellent place for a couple of hours of pottering among the rocks...

The Great Unconformity is very obvious here. While there's none of the overlying chalk, the yellow Greensand was the first sea-bottom that cut across England. It forms the golden cap of Golden Cap, and also of Thorncombe Beacon to the east of Seatown. Away in the west, at Sidmouth, that Cretaceous sea cut into red mudstones of the Permian age; here it lies over grey clays of the Jurassic.

Below Golden Cap, the Green Ammonite Beds are – disappointingly – ordinary grey. But they do contain ammonites! About 15 minutes of knocking apart fallen clay lumps yielded the two shown in the book's Introduction. Burrowing into the clay is also popular, although the amount of fallen material makes it obvious that the clay cliffs are not altogether stable.

About 400 metres west from Seatown, the Belemnite Stone is a slightly firmer grey mudstone at the very foot of the cliff. It's mostly covered over by rubble from above or shingle movement on the beach. Once found, it is liberally dotted with belemnites, like sections of badly-sharpened pencils. They

The Belemnite Stone, Seatown

are the internal shells of squid-like creatures. Sifting through beach shingle can also yield ammonite fragments, belemnites, gastropods (whelks) and crinoid segments.

From about 400 metres east of Seatown, a narrow band called the Junction Bed runs high across the cliff face. This intensely shelly pale grey limestone forms quite different beach pebbles from the chert and flint that make most of the beach.

Two geological periods (Jurassic below, Cretaceous Greensand above) not enough? Dorset Council has helped out here. Massive sea-defence boulders immediately west of Seatown appear to be Devonian Limestone from the Torbay area. They have 2cm-wide coral cross-sections.

95

WALK 12
Bridport to Seatown

Start/Finish	West Bay SY 465 905 or small pay and display at Chideock SY 423 928
Distance	15km (9 miles); or shorter version 13km (8 miles)
Ascent	450m (1500ft); or shorter version 400m (1400ft)
Approx time	4½hrs; or shorter version 4hrs
Terrain	town and village, inland hill, deeply sunken hollow way; grassy cliff tops
Maps	Explorer 116 Lyme Regis; Landranger 193 Taunton
Parking	long-stay pay and display at West Bay former station east of B3157; or small pay and display beside river in Chideock

A good 5km of airy cliff tops, and rock face investigations at Seatown, Eype's Mouth and West Bay – at least one of them ought to yield an ammonite or two. But that's just the walk's return leg. The old town at Bridport is pretty in the same golden-stone way as the Cotswolds. Fuddle your brains at the Palmers' Brewery and then sharpen them up again with the intellectual rigours of the Bridport Museum.

But what really sets this one apart is an out-of-world experience arising from being sunken below it by 10m. Shutes Lane, at the back of Symondsbury, is Dorset's slot canyon, an eroded road or hollow-way with a green and faded-orange Jurassic atmosphere.

GREENSAND

middle Jurassic

Forest Marble

Inferior Oolite

Bridport Sands

upper Lias

Charmouth Mdstn

Leave the car park at its southwest corner, and head west to **West Bay** harbour. Cross the river bridge at the back of the harbour, and turn right into a large caravan park. Head up between the caravans alongside the **River Brit**, with a tarmac path leading to a gate at the north corner of the site.

A field path runs north up the valley. It passes underneath **A35**, then to the right of a tall house. Here turn right, between stone gateposts to a path alongside

River Brit. ▶ Opposite is the **Palmers' Brewery** with its waterwheel.

> The gateposts are made from Portland Roach, with curly 'Portland Screw' fossils.

> **Palmers' Brewery** is Britain's only thatched brewery and at 200 years one of the oldest. The waterwheel from 1879 still turns but its only mechanical function is extracting cash from tourists – brewery tours are on weekdays at 11am.

Cross the street and continue left of the river, past an inexpensive car park, to a footbridge. Cross the river and head to **Bridport Church** whose walls are made from Inferior Oolite with fossil shells.

Pass the church into South Street, Bridport's main street. Turn left, passing the museum on your right, up to the Information Centre. Turn left again onto the **B3162**

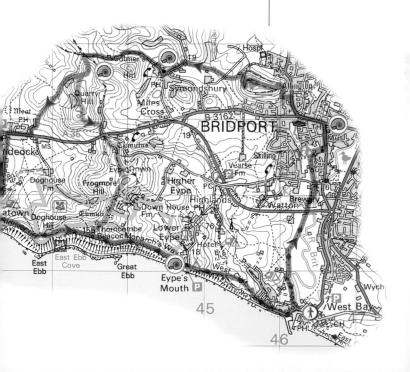

45

46

Forest Marble paving slabs (dark grey, shelly) are here and there on the left-side pavement.

(West Street). ◀ Cross the River Brit to a mini roundabout. Here turn right, along North Allington.

After 300 metres, look out for a tarmac path up to the left, with a small footpath sign – it's opposite a building marked 'Reform Place 1835 Vox Populi Vox Dei'. Head up, then leftwards, then upwards again at a street end, into woods at the base of **Allington Hill**.

At a path T junction turn right for 50 metres, then take a path back to the left, up through trees then a sunken path onto the ridge of Allington Hill. A cleared path through very rough grassland leads to the summit at the hill's western end.

Take either path ahead (they rejoin), down southwest at first. Take the first path turning down to the right, slanting northwest, to meet the perimeter path running around the base of the hill. Cross this path diagonally, and in a few steps turn down to the left, west, alongside enclosed woods, to a splitting gate at the foot of the woods.

Cross the middle of the field ahead to a gateway (ignore a tarred track over on your left here). Through the gateway follow the left edge, next to a stream, for a short distance to a footbridge. Continue through fields to left of the stream, crossing the driveway of a stone house. After two more fields, cross the stream at an old brick sheep-wash alongside a lane.

The **sheepwash** dates back to the sheep boom during the Napoleonic Wars: cleaner wool fetched better prices. It was extended in brick in the 1960s, for use as a pesticide sheepdip – an environmentally unsound one, filled by and discharging into the stream.

Turn left along the lane into **Symondsbury** (pronounced Simmonsbry). It's a very pretty village with honey-coloured houses made of inferior oolite. There's a café in an old milking shed beside the tithe barn, worth stopping at for the stonework alone.

After the church turn right, to pass Shutes Farm. The street turns into a deeply incut sunken path between

SYMONDSBURY'S INFERIOR OOLITE

The soft Bridport Sands are a poor material for buildings. The Inferior Oolite, which lies on top, is the same golden orange, but full of shelly fossils (and the occasional ammonite), and altogether more solid. It makes honey-coloured houses in Bridport, Symondsbury and indeed wherever it occurs, northwards into the Cotswolds. This tougher stone forms the tops of Allington Hill and Quarry Hill, which accordingly are lumpy with old quarries.

Stonework, Symondsbury. Inferior Oolite with shell above 'damp course' Forest Marble

And the name? It's Inferior only because it occurs lower down in the rock layers than the Great Oolite – the stone that built Bath but doesn't actually occur in Dorset. And oolite is sandstone made up of tiny rounded limestone grains like fish eggs (see Walk 16).

It's better than the Bridport Sands, but being a sandstone the oolite is still somewhat porous. In Symondsbury's older buildings the tough, grey, very shelly Forest Marble has been used for the lowest courses for damp-proofing.

SHUTES LANE

The country northwest of Bridport is the same as East Cliff (Walk 13): Inferior Oolite above Bridport Sands, with mixed sandstone of the Upper Lias below. Shutes Lane runs through the Thorncombe Sands of the Upper Lias. They are soft enough for about two centuries of graffiti, while hooves, feet and wheels have worn the track down about 10m into the bedrock. One or two oval lumps like giant rugby balls stick out of the rocky walls: these are dogger concretions (see Walk 19). Trees close overhead for a green ferny gloom.

In *Rogue Male*, the 1930s thriller by Geoffrey Household, for about half the book the hero holes out (literally) in the side of just such a sunken lane, situated in exactly this corner of Dorset (Chideock is mentioned as the nearby village). The book is in the same genre as John Buchan's *The Thirty-nine Steps* but a bit grimmer.

Shutes Lane, one of west Dorset's sunken lanes or 'holloways'

Ahead, Hell's Lane is similarly atmospheric, but muddy, rutted by motorbikes, and with dangly brambles.

bare rock walls – a dramatic Dorset holloway called Shutes Lane. It gradually rises to a crossroads at **Quarry Cross**. ◄

Turn back left sharp left, to a gate on the right, which opens onto the grassy slopes of **Quarry Hill**. A green track leads up the left flank to a humpy summit of old quarries. Bear right across this humpy ground to a small gate at the back right corner.

Short cut via Eype Down

Quarry Hill and Eype Down make a fine high ridgeline with views east over Bridport and west to Golden Cap. But you skip Seatown. Seatown's belemnites could wait for when you do Walk 10 – but it is a pity to miss out on the crab salad at the Anchor Inn.

Go through the small gate on **Quarry Hill**, to follow a waymark that marks a small path south across the hilltop (this public footpath does not appear on maps). Once across the flat, wide summit, keep south through grassed-over quarry workings, where a few lumps of orange Inferior Oolite are still lying about.

At the south edge of the hilltop, a green track runs down briefly south, then bends left to rake down towards a white building alongside the A35. Turn down right through a gate, onto a track which joins a lane to the col at the top of the **A35**. The busy road crossing has good sight lines, and traffic from both sides is climbing in low gear.

Cross the A35, bearing right into a house driveway, to a path on the left signposted 'Eype Down'. Follow any path along the scrubby hilltop, and up a brief rise to **Eype Down**'s 155m summit.

A wide path leads down, through a wood of small sycamores, to a stile and metal National Trust sign. Keep ahead along the hill ridge, with the wood edge just to your left, to a stile and signpost onto open downland. The beacon basket of **Thorncombe Beacon** is on the skyline 300 metres ahead. After visiting it, you'll return on the main route below, beneath this stile.

Don't go through the small gate, but turn right, down the steep side of the hill, with a hedge to your left. A clump of tall ash trees in the hedge stands above a stile.

Eype Down, from Thorncombe Beacon

Contour out around the field beyond. As Chideock comes into sight, slant down right a little, to a stile over a fence. Cross the narrow field behind, to another pair of stiles.

Head down the dry valley below, with a tree clump just up to the left, to a stile and gate. Here a track starts, passing around a farm shed, where it becomes concrete. Fork left to reach the A35 at the top end of **Chideock**, pronounced Chiddock.

Take the pavement down into the village, then cross into a narrow tarmac path (to the left of a white house) with signpost 'Seatown'. Keep ahead down a lane (Mill Lane) and at its foot keep ahead down a concrete track, with caravans on the left. Past the caravan site shop, join the road above Anchor Inn at **Seatown**, see Walk 11.

Here the Eype Down route rejoins.

Cross a footbridge into the car park, and head up and right to the cliff top path. Follow it up to the decorative firebeacon bucket on **Thorncombe Beacon**. ◀

The official Coastal Path now heads down alongside the cliff edge, but this is steep and a bit eroded. So it's nicer to slant inland around the head of a truncated combe, with a green path alongside a hedge down the ridge of its far side. This rejoins the cliff top at a gate. The cliff top path leads gently down to **Eype's Mouth**.

EYPE'S MOUTH AND FAULT CORNER

We all like to hide our faults – and Nature's the same. West of West Bay harbour the cliffs are grey Frome Clay, with a topping of harder Forest Marble. East Cliff is quite different: yellow Bridport Sands, topped with Inferior Oolite. We may infer a major fault, displacing the rocks to bring the grey alongside the yellow. Such major faults shatter the rocks, which then erode away into river valleys and fill up with gravel and clay. So the Mangerton Fault, up-valley from West Bay to Bridport and beyond, can only be seen by its effects.

Along the shingle for 500 metres east from Eype Mouth, you reach Fault Corner. Here, unusually, a fault is out in the open. A recent (2012) landslip is on the right, but at the top left side is the fault plane itself, smoothed off by the movement of the two rock masses.

Fault Corner

The cliff top path above Fault Corner eases inland in scrub, so there's no view of this interesting western face of it. The path then follows jumbly ground along the top of the fault line, the quarrymen exploiting the faultline shattering.

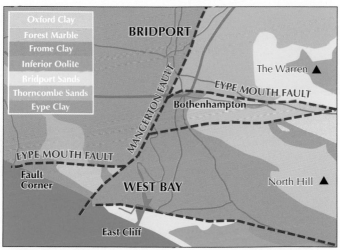

The coast path crosses the faultline itself at a stile. Here you look ahead across the River Brit (see diagram). North of Bothenhampton, the Warren is a plateau of tough Inferior Oolite above Bridport Sands and the softer Thorncombe Sands and Eype Clay. South of Bothenhampton, North Hill is a plateau of tough Forest Marble above softer Frome Clay. So the stuff to the south is a whole lot higher up the rock sequence. It's the same displacement as at Fault Corner, but carried 1km to the north by the wrench faultline north–south through Bridport.

Ammonite from Green Ammonite Beds, Seatown

Cross stepping stones above the beach, for the continuing path up the cliff rim. Above Fault Corner the path moves inland a little, through humpy quarry workings, before swinging back right to the cliff tops. Then it heads easily down to the seafront at **West Bay**. Pass around the harbour to re-cross the river bridge at its back.

WALK 13

West Bay and Burton Bradstock

Start/Finish	West Bay (harbour) SY 465 905 or at Burton Beach SY 491 889
Distance	14km (8½ miles)
Ascent	250m (800ft)
Approx time	4hrs
Terrain	good paths, tracks and streets; pathless fields on Bothenhampton Hill; tiring shingle if taking shoreline options
Maps	OS Explorer OL15 (Purbeck); Landranger 193 (Taunton)
Parking	long stay pay and display at West Bay former station east of B3157

The coastal section of this walk is quite short, about 3km, but should allow time to admire the yellow sandstone of Burton Cliff and East Cliff. They may be only 30m high, but are vertical to overhanging everywhere, and their bookshelf-like ledges are the most striking example of the Lias layering.

The inland leg of the walk includes the old centre of Bridport, plus a striking little ridgeline overlooking the town. Hyde Hill is capped with the Inferior Oolite (quarried here for Bridport buildings) and the Bridport Sands immediately beneath. Where this protection has broken away, the softer Eype Clay and other mid-Jurassic stuff erodes steeply down to near sea level.

A road bridge over the **River Brit** forms the back of the harbour. Turn off inland into a large caravan park. Head up between the caravans alongside River Brit, with a tarmac path leading to a gate at the north corner of the site. A waymarked path continues along the foot of two fields. The path then crosses an open field, to pass underneath the **A35**'s bridge.

In 200 metres, to the right of a tall, thatched house, turn right onto a smaller path signposted 'Bridport'.

middle Jurassic
Forest Marble
Inferior Oolite
Bridport Sands
upper Lias

The gateposts here are **Portland 'Roach' Stone**, see Walk 18, with the distinctive curly spiral Portland Screw fossils. A waste stone from the Portland Quarries, the Roach is often seen in field walls and sea defences; there'll be another pair of gateposts on the ridge above Bridport.

The path joins the River Brit, running upstream opposite the waterwheel on the back of **Palmers' Brewery**. Cross the street and continue left of the river, on a tarmac path alongside the Bridport football ground. After 300 metres, cross a footbridge. Keep ahead past the church of yellow Inferior Oolite to the main street.

Turn left, to the town centre and market. Before reaching the town hall, and just before the small Bridport Museum, turn off right into narrow Folly Mill Lane. At its end, turn right in Back Rivers Lane, a tarmac path, to cross a footbridge.

Ridge above Bridport

Turn right alongside the stream in Asker's Meadows, but at once bear left, signposted 'Bothenham', to **A3066** road. Cross into the lane opposite, and at a T junction turn left for 30 metres to an uphill path.

The path wiggles between houses to the foot of a field. Go straight up this to a stile, and turn right above a hedge. The path runs along the ridge crest above Hyde house (now a nursing home), passing between two gateposts again of Roach stone with casts of curly gastropod fossils. The ridgeline passes a small summit with cairn, then rises to a stile into a plateau field. The path keeps straight ahead across flat ground to a gate into a field corner. Keep ahead to another field gate at the back left corner.

Follow the fence on your left, then strike diagonally across the field to a gate at its back right corner. The hedge on your right bends round to the right, to the corner of a farm track with neglected sheds nearby. Cross the track corner to a gap into a field. ▸ Cross this diagonally southeast to exit onto a downhill track, Burbitt Lane.

The lane becomes roughly tarred as it descends towards **Shipton Gorge** (a village with exposed yellow sandstone but no gorge). As the lane bends slightly left just above the village, take a gate on the right. ▸ A field path runs southwest, along a field foot and then across

The track down right, Milvers Lane, is a possible short cut but can feature ankle-deep slurry mud.

For the New Inn, keep on down the lane to the top of the village and turn briefly up to the left.

107

four fields, with paired gates at each hedge gap – the gateways are muddy, but much less so than the farmyard on Milvers Lane above.

The path exits at a field gate with footpath signpost onto the tractor track Milvers Lane. Turn left, uphill and due south, on the firm, dry track. At the ridge top, pass to the right of a ruin and descend south into a dip. Keep ahead with hedges on your left over the crest of **North Hill**, descending to a gate. A wooded track runs down to the edge of **Burton Bradstock**.

> Old buildings in **Burton Bradstock** are of yellow Inferior Oolite, which is easy to work but slightly porous. Foundations and lower courses are often of the tough, grey, shelly and waterproof Forest Marble.

Bear right then left, following Middle Street to the church. Turn right in Mill Street, bending right past the village shop to join **B3157** at the Three Horseshoes Inn. Turn left, keeping ahead across a junction (Cliff Road) to a footpath signpost on the left. The path rises to a field; follow its left edge briefly, then strike across it diagonally to a path signpost.

To the right, across the field, is the Coast Path; but first, turn left through a kissing gate. The path crosses a small field diagonally. With a car park ahead, bear right to another signpost, standing just above the Hive Beach Café at **Burton Beach**. ◀

The walk could start and finish at the car park here.

> **Burton Cliff** overhangs in places, with obvious rockfall debris at its foot and cracks in the cliffs themselves. A walker was killed by a rockfall here in 2012 and the shingle below the cliffs was closed off for a year afterwards. Today, notices warn of the rockfall danger. At high tide, the shingle strip is very narrow, which would oblige any walker to pass immediately below the unstable cliffs. If the tide is lower, you could walk the shingle well out from the cliff foot, all the way back to West Bay.

Inferior Oolite above Bridport Sands, Burton Cliff

BURTON CLIFF AND EAST CLIFF

'Bridport Sands' are not on the Bridport beach (which is Chesil Beach shingle), but are the old-fashioned name for the sandstone rocks overhead. East Cliff, and all but the topmost layer of Burton Cliff, are formed of the very handsome yellow strata. Their bookshelf structure of ledges is the most striking example of the Lias 'layers' – a seesaw effect in the Jurassic climate, repeated dozens of times, caused the sea level to rise and fall as described in the Introduction to this section.

The hard layers are cemented former shell beds, burrowed by worms and shrimps. Honeycomb weathering, caused by expanding salt crystals inside the rock surface,

Wormeaten ledges, East Cliff

brings out the texture of the wormholes. The softer sandstone layers between are porous so that any upward arch (anticline) in the strata is a potential oil reservoir. The oil reservoir at Wych Farm near Corfe Castle is 900m underground in these same Bridport Sands.

The top few metres of Burton Cliff are a limestone called 'Inferior Oolite' – so called because its place in the strata is below the Great Oolite. The Inferior Oolite is actually a very superior sort of stone, being chock-full of fossils. Blocks of it on the foreshore contain abundant shells, both bivalves and curly gastropods. Belemnites

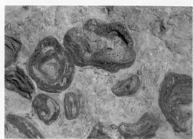

Inferior Oolite, Burton Cliff

resemble long, slender bullets; sponges are somewhat indistinct. Small ammonites are common, and ones the size of wheelbarrow tyres aren't that hard to come across.

There are also reddish blobby lumps. Known as 'snuff boxes', these are mineral concretions, dissolved iron migrating through the sedimentary rocks. Snuffboxes are complex structures, often formed around a fossil shell, and containing a kind of ancient algal slime called stromatolite, as seen at Lulworth's Fossil Forest.

From the signpost above the beach café, head inland, with the car park on your right, to a signpost where the path enters a field on the left. Cross this diagonally to another signpost (already visited, unless you chose to start at Burton Beach rather than Bridport).

Bear left, signed as Coast Path, across the field to the end of a lane (Cliff Road). The path follows the cliff tops, then descends to the corner of the bay at **Burton Freshwater**. Descend a clay bank on the left here if you want to visit the western end of Burton Cliff.

Not to be confused with River Brit at Bridport.

A path signpost stands directly opposite, across **River Bride**. ◄ The official Coast Path prefers to keep its feet dry, so it turns back sharp right through a gate. Follow

Rockfall with slabby blocks of Inferior Oolite from the cliff top, Burton Cliff west end

the stream inland for 400 metres, to cross a footbridge. Follow the stream back down, along the edge of a caravan site (with drinking water on tap), to the path signpost already spotted. ▶ Bear right, along the edge of the chalet village with the beach's shingle bank on your left, to the western corner of the bay.

If you wish to pass along below the East Cliff (even more impressive than Burton Cliff although it lacks the fossil-rich blocks of the Inferior Oolite), follow the track leading down to the shingle shore. However, for easier walking, the cliff top path slants uphill past a signpost, and follows the cliff tops, with a dip and re-climb after 400 metres. Finally the path descends steeply to the corner of **West Bay**. Bear right across the southernmost of West Bay's car park complex, with the harbour on your left.

The rivermouth has been pushed across against the foot of Burton Cliff by the eastwards march of the shingle spit.

WALK 14

Beaminster to Pilsdon Pen

Start/Finish	The Square, Beaminster ST 480 013
Distance	19km (12 miles); or field paths version 21km (13 miles)
Ascent	500m (1650ft)
Approx time	6hrs; or field path version 6½hrs
Terrain	paths, tracks and lanes – some field paths are hard to follow
Maps	Explorer 116 Lyme Regis; Landranger 193 Taunton
Parking	long stay parking a Yarn Barton, just off the Square

Pilsdon Pen at 277m is the 'traditional' high point of Dorset, while Lewesdon Hill, a couple of metres higher, is the actual high point. The outward leg of the walk is a high (for Dorset) level wander over both summits. The return is by fields and streams, through what could be considered the excessively pretty, yellow stone and thatch, village of Stoke Abbott.

After seeing the rocks out in the open in the sea cliffs, this walk is a chance to study their more subtle effects, when covered over with countryside. Hilltops here are the (Cretaceous-era) Greensand; houses are (Jurassic) Inferior Oolite.

GREENSAND
Inferior Oolite
Bridport Sands
upper Lias

From the Square, with its covered Market Cross, head down Church Lane towards the church, turning right in Shorts Lane to pass to right of the church. Keep ahead as the lane diminishes to a

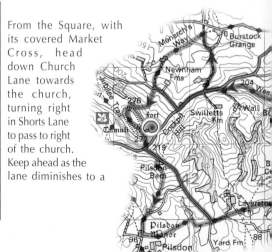

On Gerrard's Hill, view to Beominster and chalk downs

track then a field path, to join a street with an ammonite in the garage opposite.

Turn left for a few steps, then right into Halfacre Lane. After 100 metres turn off left at a footpath signpost. The path enters a field and heads up diagonally right to a gate to the right of a stone barn. ▶ At its corner turn up the left edge of a field to a small gate.

The barn is of Inferior Oolite (see Walk 12) and has shelly fossils in it.

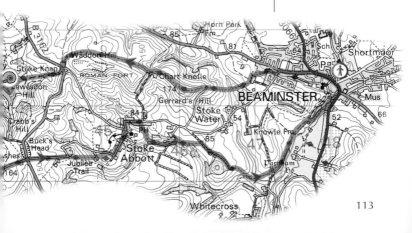

Gerrard's Hill is ahead. Head downhill through a tree belt to a footbridge, and head up over stiles to the top of **Gerrard's Hill**, with its trig point.

Descend northwest on a ridgeline to pass to the right of **Chart Knolle** house to a signpost. Keep ahead, signed 'Stoke Knapp', joining a green track running to the right away from the house. The track becomes a field path, running underneath low-voltage power lines, gently uphill across the northern flank of Chart Knolle the hill. At a gate, continue slightly left down a farm track to **Stoke Knapp** farm and the road beyond.

The old track is sunken into the Gault Clay that underlies the Greenstone cap of the hill.

Cross into a track signed for Lewesdon Hill. This bends right and heads uphill between hedges. ◄ On reaching the wooded top of **Lewesdon Hill**, turn left off the track at an iron National Trust nameplate. Head up under beech trees onto the hilltop, bearing left to its summit.

Lewesdon Hill's summit is a **cap of Greenstone**. Chert pebbles washing down the bridleway tracks off the hill form a reasonably firm path over what would otherwise be pure clay.

GREENSAND SUMMITS

The so-called Greensand is a yellowish-brown sandstone from the bed of the Chalk Sea that cuts in over the much older Bridport Sandstone below. The tough Greensand stone forms the tops of Lewesdon Hill and Pilsdon Pen, and the plateau of the Blackdown Hills away in the west. Anywhere that erosion has got through the Greensand, the softer Gault Clay

Greensand and Chert, Lewesdon Hill

and Lias rocks underneath are exposed, and the ground drops abruptly to valley level. So the hills of Greensand, flat-topped as they are, are also steep sided; too steep for pastureland, as well as being stony and sandy soil, so often growing trees. Making the Greensand as green as its name!

Away in southeast England, the Greensand is slightly tilted, and forms quite sharp ridgelines on either side of the Weald. The 170km Greensand Way, in Kent, follows the line of the southern one.

Lumps of the Greensand stone lie around on Lewesdon hill. A freshly quarried piece would indeed be greenish, but where weathered it shows yellowish brown. As it's a sea-bottom stone, it can contain seashells: usually these are dissolved out, leaving just the shell-shaped holes behind.

Along with the sandstone is smooth, whitish chert. This is a flintlike stone that forms lumps within the Greensand in the same way as flint does within the chalk: silica mineral, from fossil sponges, migrating and clumping up after the rock has formed. The chert is very tough, and can remain when the Greensand around it has eroded right away.

On Pilsdon Pen, the Greensand cap grows gorse and coarse grasses. The Gault Clay below it is waterproof, so a line of springs marks the bottom of the Greensand. Below this, the Gault itself is more fertile with grass and in early summer orchids.

Turn back sharply right (northwest) on a path along the top of steep, wooded slopes dropping to the left. After leaving the wood at another NT marker, the small path leads down the scrubby ridgeline, joining bridleway tracks at the bottom. Keep ahead on a hedged trackway (Lewesdon Hill Lane). The track reaches a minor road, **B3164**, where you keep ahead towards Pilsdon Pen.

Field path route

This avoids 1km of road by way of 2km of field paths and tracks – the field paths have no special merit so only do this if the road is busy or you really dislike roads... After 300 metres, turn down right on a concrete farm track signposted for Burstock. Keep ahead in a hedged track downhill. After 600 metres, the track rises to a signpost.

Turn left into a field. Head down it diagonally, aiming for a large, yellowish house with conservatory (Lower Newnham Farm). Cross a second field and a stream, and head up to the yellowish house. Just to the left of it, a fence has a waymark arrow but no stile. Cross and pass to left of the house onto its access track, and up this to a minor road – cross to a signpost for Pilsdon Pen.

Those on the straightforward road route just follow the B3164 for 500 metres, then turn right onto a smaller road for another 500 metres. Opposite the driveway for Lower Newnham Farm, turn left through a field gate signposted for Pilsdon Pen. ◀

Head up to right of a fence to a gateway, then slant up leftwards to a small gate at the field's top corner. Through this, follow a green track along one of the hill fort ditches at the rim of Pilsdon Pen. ◀ After 50 metres, turn up left through a small gate onto the NT-owned hilltop. Head back left within the hill fort to **Pilsdon Pen's** summit trig point.

A path with steps leads steeply down to Lob Gate car park on B3164. The simplest descent is to follow the minor road downhill to the left of the car park area for 1.3km.

Another field path route

This second field path is unenclosed, so has rather wider views – and is nearly 1km longer. From Lob Gate car park, follow the road downhill for just 200 metres. At **Pilsdon Barn** on the right, take a small gate to right of the driveway, and go through an arch hole in a hedge. Turn left, below the hedge, past a fibreglass unicorn. Pass above a field gate without going through it, but turn downhill just past it and below Pilsdon Barn.

Head down with a hedge to your right. At the second of two field gates, go through to the top corner of a large field. Head straight down this, aiming to the left of a farm shed at the field foot. Here there's a gate leading out onto a road.

Turn right for 300 metres, then left into a farm track. Where this bends right, keep ahead by taking a field gate on the left and crossing the field eastwards to the left-hand of two gates. Head up slightly left with a hedge on your right, following the field edge to a footbridge over a ditch. Turn right and follow the field edge as it bends left to a gate onto a road. The hedged path/stream ('Public Route to Public Path') is opposite.

Field path route rejoins here.

The hill's yellow Greensand and hard, whitish Chert show in the earth bank above the path.

Where the road bends right, turn left down a hedged path marked as 'Public Route to Public Path'. The path also operates as a seasonal stream. It leads down to a signpost. Keep ahead ('Stoke Abbott 2') to a stile, where you cross the driveway of **Laverstock Farm** and another track just beyond to a stile.

Here footpaths diverge. Keep ahead, just north of east, past a solo ash tree to a gateway gap. Bear slightly right (just south of east) to slant down the next field to a wooded stream valley. Cross a stile, and then duckboards and a footbridge, for a path with steps up through bushes and scrub to a field above. Head straight up to a gateway, and follow the fence then hedge on your left to join a road at the field top.

Bear left along the road, crossing a larger road (**B3162**) at the ridge top and descending the lane opposite as far as its sharp left bend at Brimley Farm. Pass to right of the farm cottage ahead of you, on a driveway becoming a grass track to a field corner. Head straight down the field, aiming to left of a picturesque thatched house on the slope opposite.

At the field foot a kissing gate leads to a footbridge. Pass up just to the left of the picturesque thatched house, and into a long field. A lane forms its top edge but aim for its back right corner. A gate leads onto a track to the left, joining the lane at its bend. Keep ahead, into **Stoke Abbott**.

Stoke Abbott from Gerrard's Hill

When it comes to pretty little villages, **Stoke Abbott** is as good as it gets. It is entirely built of bright yellow Inferior Oolite, from its 12th-century church right through to the 18th century. Its 'New Inn' is so called because it is only 400 years old.

The street bends right at the village hall. In another 300 metres turn right on a small concrete path, which runs down into a stream hollow. Cross a footbridge and turn left, keeping to right of the stream to cross a side-stream on another footbridge. The path continues through woods up to right of the stream, passing above a couple of houses, to meet a muddy track (there's a ford down on the left). Go straight across the track to a stile, and bear left to a hidden footbridge. Across this the path bears right, slanting gradually up from the stream to a field corner. Cross the field diagonally to a small gate, and keep ahead to cross a nice, firm track to join a soggy green one just behind it.

Turn right along the hedged green track (**Long Barrow Lane**), passing along the edge of Little Giant Wood. At the wood corner the track bends left, and exits into a field. Cross the field top for 50 metres to a footpath signpost, and turn straight down the field to a footbridge. Cross this, then pass the end of a second footbridge without crossing it. Instead bend up left to a small gate into a field above.

Cross the field slightly uphill to a small gate leading onto a stony track. Cross the track to a second gate and slant down to a stile onto another track along the field foot.

Turn left, now heading up the **River Brit**'s hollow towards Beaminster. The track ends at a field: cross this to a small gate just to the left of a cottage. Cross the driveway to the riverbank, and follow this to a footbridge. The riverside path beyond leads into the edge of **Beaminster**. Turn left to the Square at the walk start.

3 CHESIL BEACH

- Chalk fort at Eggardon
- Britain's biggest beach
- Sea views on the South Dorset Ridgeway
- Portland cliffs and quarries

Chesil Beach from Heights Hotel (Walk 18)

119

INTRODUCTION

On Corton Hill (Walk 17)

Chesil Beach is massive: a pile of pebbles that starts at the corner of West Bay, peels away from the land at Abbotsbury, and piles up 20m high against the Isle of Portland. It's also somewhat monotonous... and the loose pebbles make awkward walking.

The barrier beach itself means the sea can't get at the bedrock to make sea cliffs. That bedrock is a chunk of the middle Jurassic called the Corallian: a quite complicated mix-up of sandstone, gritstone, oolitic limestone and clay. Given that the rocks aren't actually exposed, it may be best to ignore them for now pending a revisit in Walk 19 at the very end of this section.

After a brief poke among the pebbles in Walk 16, enjoy the high line of the South Dorset Ridgeway, running just inland by hill forts and a factory-chimney style memorial to the wrong Thomas Hardy. Up there is also the place to see the scale of Chesil itself, and ponder the pebbles as they creep eastwards, or queue up behind Bridport's Jurassic Pier waiting for this short-lived obstacle to crumble away.

WALK 15

Litton Cheney and Eggardon Hill

Start/Finish	Eggardon Hill SY 549 948
Distance	14.5km (9 miles)
Ascent	500m (1650ft)
Approx time	4½hrs
Terrain	field paths and tracks, country lanes; two crossings of busy A35
Maps	Explorer OL15 Purbeck & S Dorset; Landranger 194 Dorchester
Parking	disused picnic place on Shatcombe Lane; there's also a pull-off south of the hill on the lane from Askerswell (SY 546 942) or street parking in Litton Cheney
Note	some footpath signs here are absent or damaged

In the context of Dorset, chalk is a tough sort of stone. A plateau of chalk, with its equally tough Greensand underneath it, lies over most of inland Dorset. Rivers cut through it, into the older clays, limestones and sands. But more notably, all around the edge of the plateau, erosion of the softer, older stones below undercuts the plateau edge to form a sharp escarpment.

The southeastern corner of the chalk scarp is at Eggardon Hill. And while most of the chalk plateau is farmed fields, Eggardon's hill fort means that it's preserved as ancient chalk downland. So cowslips and orchids are underfoot, as you enjoy the views across Oxford Clay lowlands and humpy Greensand hillocks to the sea.

At its midpoint, the walk dips into those lowlands to Litton Cheney, where the thatched bus shelter makes an ideal lunch stop.

From the picnic place head up Shatcombe Lane to the T junction at its top. Cross to a stile, and keep directly ahead on a field path (not the true right-of-way) south-west to a lane opposite a bridleway signpost.

Cross the lane and the field ahead to a small gate then a wide one leading onto the ramparts of

CHALK
GREENSAND
CORALLIAN
OXFORD Clay
middle Jurassic

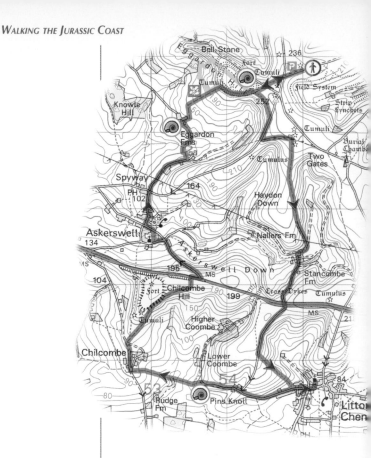

Eggardon Hill. The fort plateau is access land both sides of the fence across it.

The subtle **solufluction** structure in the combe to the south may be easier to spot when you revisit the ramparts at the end of the walk in evening light.

With only small streams (none at all on the soluble chalk), what is the force that eroded out these steepish hollows? To find out, travel 1600km north to the Tundra zone of northern Canada – or

Eggardon Coombe from the hill fort – solufluction slumps

alternatively 20,000 years back in time to the end of the Ice Age. In the brief warmth of summer, a soggy lump of soil can slide downhill over the permanently frozen ground below – the process called solufluction. The newly exposed bedrock is now exposed to thaw-and-refreeze, breaking it up, eventually, to slide away in its turn.

Return through the wide gate, and keep ahead on a green, hedged track along the rim of the Eggardon combe. Keep ahead, past a parking pull-off to a field gate on the left opposite a bridleway signpost. ▶ The field gate (it's a RUPP or road used as public path) is unsigned.

The walk could start and finish at this parking pull-off.

Follow a grassed-over tractor track above the head of Coombe Bottom to a shed and radio mast. Don't go through the gate here but turn right, down the field edge, with a hedge to your left. ▶ Cross the next field in the same direction, to the top of a track descending to **Stancombe Farm**.

You walk on pineapple weed, and on flints cleared to the field edge.

Pass to right of a large shed and up the tarmac access track of the farm to the **A35**. Cross into Chalk Pit Lane opposite. After 800 metres, with a 'steep hill' sign seen ahead, field gates are on both sides of the road (neither is signed as footpath although both are). Take the one on the left, and descend to the left of a fence. Small gates lead down past a vineyard to a valley-bottom lane. Turn left to **Litton Cheney**. ▶ Just past the thatched millennial

There is street parking to the south of the main crossroads, which provides another potential start/finish point.

bus shelter, a short side path with a turnstile, romantic and ferny, leads to the church.

From the main crossroads, take the same lane back out west, signposted for 'Askerswell'. After 1km the lane bends up right: here keep ahead, on a grass track passing below Coombefield Farm. The bridleway track passes above **Pins Knoll** and then above a bench with a view across to the Knoll and Puncknowle.

It's a bench on a **bench** – the level shelf followed by the bridleway is a bench (a landscape shelf) of Greensand, the harder bed lying underneath the Chalk. The Chalk scarp rises on your right. Across the valley ground of soft Oxford Clay, the Knoll is a remnant of Greensand no longer flat topped and soon to erode away altogether.

The track bends down right. Take the left-hand of two gates (waymarked) and drop with a hedge on your right towards the stream valley. Ignore a gate on the right with a yellow footpath arrow, but take the lower one with blue bridleway arrow at the field's bottom corner. Go down the next field past a solo oak to a footbridge in a tree belt, and straight up the field beyond. Emerge through a gateway at a lane.

Chalk downland on Eggardon Hill

FLINT AND CHERT

Ploughed fields below the chalk escarpment are littered with both flint and chert. The Greensand and chalk that form the plateau above once covered the valleys as well; these tough pebbles, so tiresome to farmers, are all that remain of those vanished rock layers.

Chert (left) and flint, in ploughed field at Chilcombe

Both flint and chert are lumps of silica, the simple mineral that makes quartz and glass. The silica probably started off as fossil fragments – flint, which is the specific chert formed in chalk, is silica that was the internal spicules of sponges. During the compression and heating of rock formation, the silica gets to wander around within the rock mass and assemble itself into these lumpy shapes. Flint is grey-black, with an off-white weathered outside. Chert from the Greensand is mostly shiny yellowish-brown, again with a paler outer layer. Away in the east, the chert formed within the Portland Limestone is dark grey, in much larger lumps than flints from the chalk.

Turn up to the right, through a short 'holloway' road cutting. At the lane's high point, a path signpost stands just beyond a track running to the right. Bear right (northeast, signposted as bridleway) across open field to a small gate among brambles. The path beyond is a hill groove slanting gently up around the slope just below **Chilcombe Hill Fort** (which is now ploughed fields) to a small gate. Cross the field beyond slightly uphill to its far hedge, and turn left alongside this over to the **A35**. Turn right, through a lay-by, then cross to a lane opposite, marked as a steep downhill.

Descend the lane to the slope foot, turning left to **Askerswell** Church and Manor Farm. ▶ From the back right (northeast) corner of the churchyard a small gate leads onto a sunken, ferny path. This emerges at a drive-way end into a lane.

The church has a 14th-century tower, the rest is a 19th-century rebuild.

Turn left to a crossroads, and up right to a T junction near **Spyway**. Cross into the tarmac driveway for Eggardon House. Follow it towards South Eggardon Farm, but just before the farm take a small gate down on the left with bridleway arrow. Pass a small ornamental pool, to wiggle right then left into a field. Slant uphill to the left above a broken hedge, through a soggy patch to a small gate. Through it, a path leads to **North Eggardon Farm**.

> A narrow outcrop of **Eggardon Grit** can be seen above and left, below the Greensand bench that extends Eggardon hill fort to the northwest. Such natural inland crags are rare in Dorset. This one is a tougher layer within the Upper Greensand that lies below the hill's chalk topping. A retaining wall below the first building of the farm displays the stone, coloured with greenish-brown glauconite mineral.

Pass below the first building, then above a large shed onto the tarmac access lane. As this bends downhill, turn right up a hedged, stony track. This soon becomes a green path up the flank of **Eggardon Hill Fort**. Where the green bridleway track bends right, keep up ahead through a gate and up the rings and ditches to the rim of the hill fort. Follow the rim to the right, to the gate out of the fort passed on the outward route. Through the gate retrace the first steps of the walk back to the picnic pull-off.

WALK 16

Abbotsbury Castle and Chesil Beach

Start/Finish	Abbotsbury SY 578 852
Distance	18km (11 miles); or shorter version 13km (8 miles)
Ascent	300m (1000ft); or shorter version 250m (800ft)
Approx time	5hrs; or shorter version 4¼hrs
Terrain	paths, mostly very good but faint field paths around Swyre
Maps	OS Explorer OL15 Purbeck; Landranger 194 Dorchester
Parking	pay and display village car park on B3157 at east end of Abbotsbury

A graded heap of shingle, 29km long and 15m high, weighing 100 million tonnes. It's an extraordinary bit of natural stone-shifting, unique in Europe.

On the other hand, 29km may be more shingle spit than you really want to walk past... This walk gives you just 6km of it, and then an overview from the Greensand ridgeline inland and 200m above.

From the car park head in through the village, past side roads down left and back right, to the village store on the left. Here a track turns off. Follow it downhill to a junction (coast path turns right) and up the path ahead to **St Catherine's Chapel**.

GREENSAND
Kimmeridge Clay
CORALLIAN
OXFORD Clay
middle Jurassic
Forest Marble

St Catherine's Chapel, Abbotsbury

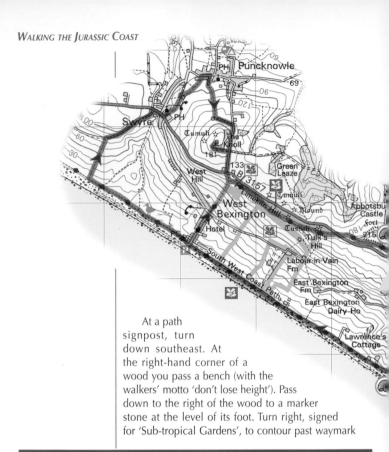

At a path signpost, turn down southeast. At the right-hand corner of a wood you pass a bench (with the walkers' motto 'don't lose height'). Pass down to the right of the wood to a marker stone at the level of its foot. Turn right, signed for 'Sub-tropical Gardens', to contour past waymark

OOLITE LIMESTONE

Abbotsbury and St Catherine's Chapel are built of oolite limestone, the Osmington Oolite, part of the Corallian formation. (The Abbey, however, is of paler Portland Stone.) Oolite is formed from the kind of limestone sand that makes the white beaches of the Bahamas. A peculiarity of calcite (the limestone mineral) is that it is less soluble in hotter water. Hence the limescale in your kettle. Thus also in shallow tropical seas, calcite precipitates out around particles of shell or grit, to form tiny, rounded sand grains – these are the ooids, egg-things, although each egglet is scarcely visible to the naked eye.

Oolites make good building stone. Dorset oolites vary from cream to orange, depending on the iron content. Good building stone is fossil-free, but stone used in field barns and walls may be more rewarding. The Inferior Oolite is made into Dorset villages wherever a quarry of it's close enough. The Great Oolite does not occur in Dorset, but the city of Bath is built of it. Dorset's most famous building stone, Portland Stone, is also an oolite.

When discussing oolite, pronounce the two Os separately – oh-olite.

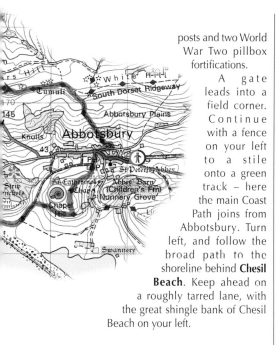

posts and two World War Two pillbox fortifications.

A gate leads into a field corner. Continue with a fence on your left to a stile onto a green track – here the main Coast Path joins from Abbotsbury. Turn left, and follow the broad path to the shoreline behind **Chesil Beach**. Keep ahead on a roughly tarred lane, with the great shingle bank of Chesil Beach on your left.

Lumps of **Portland Stone** stop cars from driving onto the beach shingle. Many carry fossil shells, and some have the distinctive spiral gastropods called Portland Screws. Confusingly, one or two of the beach-block stones are chalk or flinty silcrete.

CHESIL BEACH

Chesil, a graded heap of shingle, 29km long and 15m high, starts at the Jurassic Pier, West Bay. At Abbotsbury it detaches itself from the land, to shut off a sheltered sea strip called the Fleet. After 14km of unattached existence it bangs up against the Isle of Portland – which was a true island until the shingle spit hit it.

The simple process that forms it is called Longshore Drift. With prevailing winds from the south-west, every wave pushes a pebble up the beach with a slight nudge towards Portland. The backwash sucks it back again directly down-slope.

While it's unsurprising that such nudges, repeated over 10,000 years, should sort the pebbles into

Chesil Beach, at Cogden Beach

sizes, it's not understood precisely why this results in pea-sized pebbles at West Bexington, uniformly increasing to baked-potato size ones at the Isle of Portland.

Over 20,000 years since the Ice Age, 60 billion wave nudges have moved pebbles to Portland from Budleigh Salterton and beyond. When a migrating pebble reaches an impassable headland, it sits and waits for an ice age to start or to end, as this gives a convenient change in sea level. On a smaller scale, in bays such as Budleigh Salterton and Seaton, migrating shingle spits have forced the emerging river to the extreme eastern edge of the bay. The pebbles of Chesil are mostly flint (from chalk) and chert (from Greensand), but also include the distinctive reddish-brown Budleigh Salterton quartzite discs. There's no way today that pebbles can get nudged around the many rocky headlands between Budleigh and West Bay: to understand the beach we have to unravel the various changes in sea level since the end of the Ice Age, 20,000 years ago.

With obstacles including the Jurassic Pier at West Bay preventing any fresh shingle from the west, Chesil is gradually shortening. It may lose 3km over the next 10–20 years, to start only at Burton Beach (Walk 13). As well as moving eastwards, Chesil Beach is migrating inland at about 5cm per year. West of West Bexington, shingle migrating onto the path makes for tiresome walking here and there.

The rough track continues along the back of Chesil Beach, to the beach car park below **West Bexington**.

Short cut through West Bexington
The longer route gives a bit more Chesil Beach, the village of Swyre plus two pubs, and an add-on viewpoint at the Knoll. This no-frills short cut is simpler: just Chesil Beach, and the airy ridgeline overhead.

Head inland, up the road past the Manor Hotel to a T junction. Here keep ahead up a rough stony hedged track. At the foot of a wood, take the track bearing right. Re-joining the longer route, it runs up to join **B3157** at a lay-by.

Beyond the seaside car park, continue along the shoreline path. On the right are reeds of a nature reserve: formerly open water like the Fleet. After 1.5km, at a signpost, the path turns right over a footbridge. Ignore a signpost for Swyre, and continue left along a narrow field with a hedge on its left separating it from the sea. After 200 metres look out for a waymarked gate over on your right.

Head uphill, with a wide thorn-belt hedge on your right, to a gateway gap onto a tractor track (New Lane). Turn right, to reach B3157 at the edge of **Swyre**.

Turn right across a bridge, and immediately before the Bull Inn turn left on a hedged-in path. After 300 metres you pass a yellow cottage; immediately after it take a stile on the right. Contour across a bottom corner of the field to a hedge corner, and keep on in the same direction across another corner to a stile in front of houses. A path leads between them to the street in **Puncknowle**.

Ahead up through the village are the small church and 16th-century Crown Inn.

Turn right to a junction. ◄ The walk route continues up the track on the right, signed for Knackers Hole. After about 100 metres, a sign points left, into a belt of trees. The path runs up in this tree belt, quite muddy and awkward, to emerge to a narrow field above. Head up this to a signpost and a field track running to the left. It leads out to a lane (Clay Lane) high on Puncknowle's Knoll.

Turn right, across the hill crest. At the lane's highest point, a stile on the right leads to a green track that winds up to the small disused hut (and bench) at **The Knoll** summit. The hut has a weatherproof roof and the views are very wide.

The short cut, and S Dorset Ridgeway, rejoin here.

Return to the lane, and follow it on down to **B3157**. Cross and turn down left, signposted for West Bexington. In 100 metres, take a track back up to the left, to rejoin B3157 at a lay-by. ◄

From the lay-by end, a path continues along **Limekiln Hill**, with the road nearby on the left and scrubby ground falling to the right. After 400 metres, the path turns slightly uphill at a waymark post, with the top of a limekiln immediately below. The path crosses a tumulus, and joins the road at a footpath signpost.

Cross diagonally, for a path continuing to the trig point of **Abbotsbury Castle** (Abbotsbury Hill Fort on signposts).

The Knoll and Abbotsbury Castle are capped with **Greensand**: a shelly sandstone that is actually yellowish when weathered. Path stones on Abbotsbury Castle, and masonry of a fallen wall, show the shelly sealife of the Greensand Sea, which cut across the Dorset landmass at the start (or bottom) of the Cretaceous, and later developed into the sludgy Chalk Sea.

An east–west faultline has raised the tough Greensand, along with underlying Jurassic rocks such as the Forest Marble. To the north is chalk country, with its softer contours: this chalk brought downwards by the fault (Abbotsbury Fault) to lie alongside the older and tougher Greensand of the ridge.

From the trig point keep ahead through a gate and a ring of earthworks to cross a minor road. Just beyond is a beacon basket, and the lower half of some hut, clad in blocks of Greensand with shelly fossils and traces of wormholes. Views are right along Chesil Beach to the Isle of Portland.

The wide path follows the airy ridgeline, along the top of the drop towards the sea. After 1.2km you pass though a gate above a combe corner (with a small fish pool in the valley floor directly below). Here the path forks. Bear right, on a green path around the rim of the combe, then down through a small rocky outcrop (cherty Greensand) to a wide field gate in a hedge. Go straight down the field below to a small gate at the corner of a fence. Below this a grassy track starts to form, with scrubby ground up on its left. It becomes a hedged stony track. ▶ The track drops to **Abbotsbury**, arriving in Back Lane. Turn right to the crossroads at the village centre.

Descending to Abbotsbury from the South Dorset Ridgeway

Bare yellow rock shows in its bed at one point, the Abbotsbury Ironstone.

WALK 17

Hardy Monument to Elwell

Start/Finish	Hardy Monument, west of Dorchester SY 613 876
Distance	14.5km (9 miles)
Ascent	300m (1000ft)
Approx time	4½hrs
Terrain	tracks and paths; some paths very faint or absent
Maps	Explorer OL15 Purbeck; Landranger 194 Dorchester
Parking	at Hardy Monument or at Smitten Corner 400 metres down east

Hardy's Monument is mildly surprising, twice. In this chalk country it stands among lime-hating heather; and in this country dedicated to Thomas Hardy, it actually commemorates a quite different Tom Hardy, Nelson's flag captain at the Battle of Trafalgar ('Kiss me, Hardy' being Nelson's dying words). It's built of good local stone, even if it does look like a factory chimney.

From this high viewpoint two downland ridges run eastwards to the A354 at Ridgeway Hill. The northern (chalk) one, used for the outward walk, is well tracked and carries the South Dorset Ridgeway. The southern (Portland Stone) one is smaller but steeper, with the inconspicuous Jubilee Trail created by the Ramblers' Association.

> Tertiary gravel
> CHALK
> PORTLAND
> Kimmeridge Clay

Opposite the **Hardy Monument** car park entrance, a signposted path runs downhill to rejoin the road below. There's more car parking here (Smitten Corner), beside a forest track with barrier on the left. Opposite that track, take a stony, unsignposted track on the right.

The track, fenced on both sides then just on the right, runs southeast along **Bronkham Hill** ridge crest with tumuli.

More recent flinty **river gravel** overlies the chalk. Where caverns within the chalk have collapsed are now shake holes, circular hollows mostly growing nettles. There is also a small pothole, rimmed with unstable gravel sediments, and used by the farmer as a dump for fence wire.

Map continues on page 136

These chalk-free river gravels account for the heathy vegetation around Hardy's Monument. They are of Tertiary Period, the Bagshot Beds, and are best seen in old quarries around the monument. The river system that formed them was a big one, as among their flints the beds have quartz from Dartmoor granite and jasper from Cornwall.

After nearly 2km the track bends gently to the left (east) and becomes a wide path down through gorse. After crossing a concrete track, the bridleway becomes a sequence of field edges along the eastward ridgeline. The fence is on your right. After 500 metres a signpost indicates a line leftwards away from the fence to a gate

Horse riders east of Hardy's Monument

135

to the left of a tumulus. Through this continue with fencing on your right. After a gate between two reservoir-like tumuli (no, actually tumulus-like reservoirs), the faint path becomes a track. This runs down to **B3159** road.

Opposite, take the tarmac track, which reverts to chalky stone, over a low rise and down. Approaching the gap at **Ridgeway Hill** and the new **A354**, the wide, white stony track bends right. Keep round right into a descending, hedged track (the road before the old A354, itself before the wide new road in its cutting). Cross a track (left, it leads to the former A354 now bike trail). In another 100 metres bear right in a grass path alongside the old sunken track. ◄ It descends to a track junction at the edge of **Elwell** village with the village street just below.

Or stay in the sunken track to reach Ship Inn at its foot. Turn right on the narrow lane just below the inn to rejoin the Jubilee Trail.

Jubilee Trail waymarks will guide for the rest of the walk. Turn right, on a path that runs through small gates along a field foot above the houses of the village. Keep ahead over stone stiles among houses, across the top of a domestic garden, then out along Goulds Hill Close to **B3159** road. Turn left down this rather busy road for 50 metres to the village hall at the end of a lane to the church. Pass to left of the village hall, the Wishing Well café on your left, to a track slanting up right. Keep ahead on a path into woods.

From the stile at the wood top, slant ahead across a field to join the ridge crest, with a stile and signpost for Friar Waddon.

The **Weymouth Anticline** once rose as a wide arch of Portland Stone between here and the Isle of Portland. The higher, middle part of the arch eroded away, to expose the Kimmeridge Clays and other softer rocks below. These have washed out to form the low-lying ground to the south towards Weymouth. Meanwhile this walk heads back west along the ridgeline formed by the exposed, uptilted edge of the Portland Stone along the northern slope of the arch.

Follow the ridge crest ahead, west. After 1km cross a tarmac track and keep ahead, signed 'Corton Hill'. Keep along the ridge crest, dipping into a gap with four sets of power lines at various heights overhead. Slant slightly right to a stile onto a lane corner, but at once turn left in a concrete driveway for 40 metres, then right through a waymarked kissing gate.

The marked path doesn't follow the line marked on maps. It contours ahead, across the flank of **Corton Hill** along the foot of the steepest slope, then above a fence. From the fence corner it bears slightly downhill, to a stile to a road junction.

Turn right on the road through the gap in the ridge-line, then turn off left at a bridleway-signed track. Follow this short track up to a gate, then bear left, again sign-posted as bridleway, along a fenced field track. In 100 metres take a gate on the left, and continue in the same direction (northwest) on a grass path with fences on your

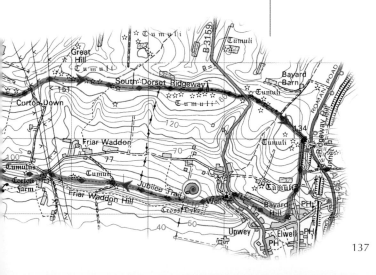

Hardy's Monument

right. Continue like this through waymarked gates, with a fence (or briefly wall) on your right, into the shallow hollow of Hell Bottom.

Pass through a gate to right of the ruined **Bench** farmhouse and modern farm sheds, and take a tractor track ahead up the valley floor to a field gate. Ahead, a groove in the field marks the old bridleway line. Follow this up through a gateway gap, and keep straight on up the field above to its top right corner. Here a gate leads onto the track along **Bronkham Hill**.

Turn left, retracing the outward route to the lower car park at Smitten Corner, and the **Hardy Monument** above.

The Hardy Monument is built of **Portland Stone**, quarried locally from the northern slope of the Weymouth Anticline. Modern repairs are with better stuff from the Portland quarries, on the anticline's southern slope. The poorer, older stone is more rewarding for finding fossils in.

WALK 18
Isle of Portland circuit

Start/Finish	New Ground, Isle of Portland SY 689 731
Distance	13.5km (8½miles)
Ascent	150m (500ft)
Approx time	4hrs
Terrain	paths (mostly wide, smooth and busy) and tracks
Maps	Explorer OL15 Portland; Landranger 194 Dorchester
Parking	follow A354 up onto plateau and turn left at a roundabout, near the Heights Hotel

The Isle of Portland is shaped by man. Its side cliffs are quarried, and so is most of its top. The whole thing is one slab of the highly desirable Portland Stone; the missing bits of the island make fine buildings all over Dorset and England, including St Paul's Cathedral. But Sir Christopher Wren turned his nose up at the bits with the ammonites, the shells and the curly snail fossils, so those are still lying about locally.

The walk follows the rim of the Portland slab, right around the island. At just one point, below the Young Offenders' Institution, it dips into the jumbly ground below the quarried cliffs.

With Chesil Beach views on your left, head to the end of the car park, and a lane beyond over a bridge (made of Portland Roach). At a lane junction keep ahead, signposted as Coast Path. The lane bends right (Coast Path signpost three ways) beside a moat bridge to the **prison**. The lane bends right again, to pass a community farm (Fancy's Farm) where it decreases to a track.

Follow the track ahead through quarries, with stone markers and waymark posts for the Coast Path. You reach a lane, with a cliff top viewpoint ahead left (where you see all along the chalk coast eastwards), and an old engine shed directly ahead: but bear right, following waymark posts, to pass along the perimeter of the **Young Offender Institution** to a tarred lane along the rim of the plateau.

PURBECK
PORTLAND
Kimmeridge Clay

With an obelisk 10 metres ahead, turn down sharp left, signed 'Coast Path', on a small, slightly rocky path. It leads through a goat-proof gate and below Portland Stone cliffs, then zigzags down towards the sea, to join a wide, smooth path, a former quarry railway.

Turn right on this path, with cliffs some way above and broken-up quarry ground down on your left. The path passes above **Durdle Pier** (a small side-path leads down to it) then along the base of low cliffs with rock climbers. Here fork left to stay below the cliffs on the main path, with the ruined **Rufus Castle** soon appearing ahead. ◄ At the base of the castle, the Coast Path bears down left. But first, a right turn up a tarmac path leads to the Portland Museum. Opening hours are rather short, but it has ammonites and a fossil tree trunk outside.

The Coast Path passes below the castle, and drops to **Church Ope Cove**. Immediately above the beach, the

Rufus Castle, built around 1080, is the earliest known building in Portland Stone.

PORTLAND ROACH

Above the main Portland Stone lies a layer that was once a shelly beach. It's full of fossils, including the curly sea snail known as the Portland Screw. (What you see are the holes in the stone where the actual seashells have dissolved away.) The stone they sit in is called the Roach.

If you're Sir Christopher Wren planning on building St Paul's, this Aero-bar upper layer of the Portland Stone has to be quarried away to

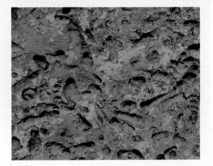

Portland Stone, on the Cobb at Lyme Regis; with Portland Screw gastropods

get at the good Portland Freestone underneath. As a cheaper waste stone, the Roach is used for sea defences, field walls and gateposts. It was also used for Victorian forts, as the many small holes made it good at absorbing cannon balls.

path passes along the backs of beach huts, then up stone steps, to continue along quarry terraces above the sea. After 400 metres the path bends back up right to join a road above.

Turn left along the verge, passing Cheyne Weares car park on the cliff top, then the Coast Path (signposted) forks off left on a short track becoming a path. This runs along quarry terraces above the sea. The route is now straightforward, on wide paths along the tops of low sea cliffs, past several old cranes, one of them standing above a spectacular sea cave.

Pass along the seaward side of beach huts, and pass the Lobster

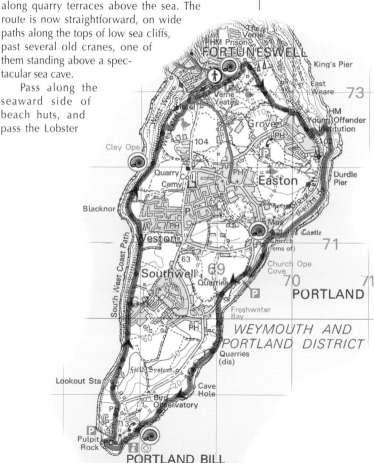

141

Café and lighthouse, to the Trinity House pyramid at the tip of **Portland Bill**.

> The level ground at the south end of Portland is a **raised beach**, cut off by the sea at a time after the Ice Age when the sea level was about 10m higher than today. East of the Lobster Café you can find beach shingle and seashells from that time, cemented together with calcite mineral.

Follow the low cliff tops around, past **Pulpit Rock** (the leaning slab has carved footholds for scramblers). Ahead is a fenced MoD compound. Pass around the inland side of this, with a large car park on your right, and cross the compound's access track near a coast path signpost. Head up the grassy slope beyond to pass the **lookout station** at the top.

Sea stack at Southwell

The coast path now follows west-facing cliff tops. It passes outside Southwell's industrial estate, then the

corner of **Weston** above Mutton Cove. ▶ At **Blacknor** point, the path passes to seaward of a walled and ugly circular house, and becomes quite narrow and exposed.

Ancient sea bed ripples are seen in the Purbeck Limestone surface just down left of path.

West Cliff is Portland Stone above, but Portland Sands (sandstone and clay-lime marls) below; and below them is Kimmeridge Clay. The softer Portland Sands have slipped away downhill. Just above the sea, greyish marl beds have been tipped upwards like the foot of a ski jump.

On the cliff top here, the **Memo Project** may rise in 2017, a sculptural building commemorating all the species lost in Earth's sixth great mass extinction, the one currently being caused by mankind.

In 2013, a short section (about 400 metres) of path was closed with a waymarked diversion just inland through lumpy quarry ground. The path then passes through a masonry arch, to reach a further closed section. Here the waymark posts inland lead in 50 metres to a clump of sculptures. Bear left to join a wide, smooth path, passing many more sculptures – this is the right-of-way line on maps. At a T junction, the coast path diversion turns left.

An interpretation board with a **sculptures** key is on the right. One of them, pictured but unmapped, is Antony Gormley's 'Still Falling'. To find it, look around for more scrambled-looking Purbeck Stone forming the highest nearby lump of ground. Continue past the interpretation boards to fork right, and keep right to pass to right of the slightly-higher Purbeck lump, to find the sculpture on your left, below the Purbeck/Portland boundary.

From the interpretation board the Coast Path diversion returns to the cliff top path, turning right on the main Coast Path, to reach a corner of the **A354** road at an old crane.

Fossil tree at Heights Hotel

Ammonites are in its roadside wall, and fossil tree chunks are dotted around the lawn, plus a large lump of travertine flow stone.

Cross to a path with handrail, and head up it, with Chesil Beach views over Fortuneswell. Turn right up a lane to the Heights Hotel. ◀ Bear left to a war memorial, with the car parks of Old Ground just behind it.

144

WALK 19
Osmington shore and White Horse

Start/Finish	Preston, bridge over River Jordan SY 703 830
Distance	14.5km (9 miles); or shorter version 13km (8 miles)
Ascent	350m (1200ft)
Approx time	4½hrs; or shorter version 4hrs
Terrain	paths and tracks; a steep grass descent off Chalbury
Maps	Explorer OL15 Purbeck; Landranger 194 Dorchester
Parking	side streets in Preston; also Smugglers' Inn at Osmington Mills, and expensive parking at Bowleaze Cove

A walk combining chalk downland with Jurassic seaside – the special features being the jolly looking white horse carved into West Hill, and the ammonite hunting at Redcliff Point. Although the walk is fairly short, the Smugglers' at Osmington Mills could delay you over a long lunchtime; and so could the foreshore below it, with lots more fossils and the bizarre 'dogger' concretions.

Just west of the bridge over the **River Jordan**, take the small Mill Lane past the Bridge Inn. It becomes an enclosed footpath, to a street corner. Keep ahead for 300 metres, continuing into a track ahead as the street bends right.

After 30 metres, and before a track tee ahead, look for a footpath signpost in the hedge on your left. Follow a field's left edge to a corner at the edge of Preston's back gardens, turning right and uphill along the field edge. There are views of the white horse. At the field top take a track ahead, passing to the left of a covered reservoir then bending right towards the earthworked Chalbury Hill. After a cattle grid, leave the track to head up onto the summit of **Chalbury Hill**.

Take a small path down north. As the slope steepens, slant slightly left, to a stile onto the Combe Valley

CHALK
GREENSAND
PURBECK
PORTLAND
Kimmeridge Clay
CORALLIAN
OXFORD Clay

Road. Turn right along the lane for 150 metres, then cross the second of two stiles on the right, signposted for Osmington and waymarked as South Dorset Ridgeway.

A grass path bends around the base of **Green Hill** (which is up on its left) to a stile back onto the same road. Turn left for just 50 metres. A track on the right runs up onto West Hill, with hedges above it and wide views below.

After 1km, emerge through a gate with a ruin in the undergrowth on your left. Keep ahead, passing to the right of one tumulus and to the left of the next, to a gate with signpost. Bear right up the fenced track beyond, crossing the highest point of **White Horse Hill** with a trig point in the field to your right.

The track ends at a gate. Continue along the top edge of an open field to another gate, with a signpost just beyond.

Where the track becomes tarmac at the start of the village, a path back right, signed for Sutton Poyntz', could be followed for 200 metres for a much better view of the hill carving.

Short cut to Osmington

Here a signed track forks down right for Osmington. It crosses the valley floor, with a glimpse back right of the Osmington White Horse. ◄ Follow the lane ahead up into **Osmington**. Take the first lane on the left (Village Street) and turn right (Chapel Lane) now back on the main route up to **A353**.

Osmington White Horse

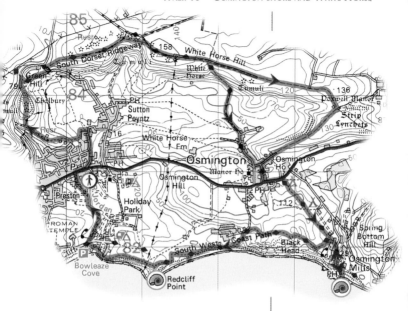

Continue along the field top. After a gate, follow the fenced path ahead along the crest. It develops into a wide green track, to a gate under phone masts.

Through the gate bear right to another gate, and a track running across a shallow valley to a track junction behind farm sheds (Pixon Barn). Turn right on this stony track, which runs down a gentle ridgeline towards Osmington. Where the track bends left, keep ahead in a wide gravel path under trees, which leads down to a street corner in **Osmington**. Here turn left up Chapel Lane. ▶

At the main **A353** turn left (east) out of the village, passing a plastic cow on your right. As the road bends left, a footpath on the right is signposted for Osmington Mills. Follow it over a footbridge, then uphill from gate to gate with hedges on your left. At the slope top continue straight down a field to a gate under a low-voltage power line. Keep ahead alongside the hedge on your left to the field's bottom left corner.

The short cut route rejoins here.

147

OSMINGTON DOGGERS

Imagine a circulating crowd of all sorts of people: Goths, Old Etonians, geologists. When two Old Etonians bump into each other, they tend to clump together. The same happens under the pressure and heat of rock formation. Various minerals are liberated to wander around within the sandy mass.

Dogger concretions, Osmington Mills

When they meet their own kind they cling together in chemical combination. The resulting lumps are called 'concretions'.

Concretions formed by migrating calcite, the limestone mineral, make smooth, near-spherical lumps called doggers, anything up to a metre across. See them sticking out of the eroding cliff side west of Osmington Mills, or simply lying about on the foreshore.

Diversion to Osmington Mills

Here, if you want a look at the strange spheroidal doggers and abundant shelly fossils, a hedged-in path to the left takes you to a lane above **Osmington Mills**. Turn downhill to the Smugglers' Inn. Head round to the left of the inn, for an enclosed path into fields, where a gate on the right and steps down lead to the foreshore. The diversion takes about 10mins; allow another hour for explorations.

To continue towards Bowleaze Cove, turn right in a hedged path up the field edge, signposted for Weymouth. Follow the coast path through wooded landslip ground, then along grassy slopes above the sea. Pass a first side path down left towards Redcliff Bay, and then pass below Osmington Bay Holiday Centre. A solar powered shower stands at the top of a second path down to the bay. ◄ The coast path runs along the seaward edge of a field, and up to a bench above **Redcliff Point**.

Head down this path for ammonite hunting in the grey mudstone of Redcliff Point.

Scallop in Corallian limestone, Redcliff Point

REDCLIFF POINT

Redcliff Point

The unspectacular low cliffs of Redcliff Point are a mixture of yellowish Corallian, with scallop-type shells, and grey mudstone of the Oxford Clays. This grey rock holds ammonites, up to 5cm across. Look for angular lumps of the more solid rock, rather than mere clay – you may see piles of chippings where previous ammonite-fanciers have been at work. The rock can be gently prised apart without any hammering. Further west, the yellower sandstone has slipped down over the grey clay and mudstone, with the coast path passing above the distinctive scoops and hollows of landslipped terrain.

Ammonite in Oxford Clay, Redcliff Point

The path runs down towards the beach complex at **Bowleaze Cove**. It reaches the cove to left of the buildings, then bends around the corner of the blue Riviera Hotel. Past a funfair, keep ahead to slant across a car park and cross a road to a gravel path ahead.

The path runs through fields, bending left then right, before running into Weymouth Bay Holiday Park. Keep ahead between the caravans to a little roundabout, and continue ahead on a tarmac path signed for the Spar shop, to emerge from the holiday park entrance to the A353 in the middle of **Preston**. Turn right for 200 metres to the bridge over River Jordan.

4 CHALK WALKS
Lulworth and inland

- A rude man at Cerne Abbas
- Dorset's chalk downs
- Smugglers' path to White Nothe
- Lulworth Cove's fossil forest

Bats Head (Walk 24)

INTRODUCTION

Coast Path at Bran Point (Walk 23)

During the Chalk time, as now, there was no Arctic continent; but there was no Antarctica either, and no great icecaps to lock away some of the sea. So sea levels were higher then, by about 200m. And the sea swept in across England, and much of western Europe, chopping off the older layers below in the Great Unconformity (see Introduction).

Paleogeographers are people who track the moving continents backwards through the ages. They tell us that the shallow Cretaceous sea was shut in by land, and lacked cleaning currents. That sea's first sediments form the Greensand, its green tinge making it a rock of a stagnant, low-oxygen sea floor.

What comes on top of that is the residue of an unprecedented ecosystem. Green algae bloomed through that warm, stagnant sea. They dropped their calcite skeletons, each grain the size of a pinprick, over 30 million years, to form a layer of white, featureless limestone several hundred metres thick: the Chalk.

The chalk plateau, cut about as it is by river valleys, stretches across most of north and western Dorset – and onwards via the Chilterns to the downs of Lincolnshire and east Yorkshire. Its interior gives walking of a bleak and flinty sort; its sudden edge gives green and lively lowlands. At Lulworth, and again at Old Harry in the book's final section, chalk stands high in fine, exciting cliff tops.

WALK 20

Cerne Abbas and the Giant

Start/Finish	Minterne Magna ST 659 043
Distance	21.5km (13½ miles); or shorter version 14.5km (9 miles)
Ascent	300m (900ft); or shorter version 250m (800ft)
Approx time	6hrs; or shorter version 4hrs
Terrain	tracks and paths
Maps	Explorer 117 Cerne Abbas; Landranger 194 Dorchester
Parking	car park on A352 opposite church and Minterne Magna garden

The Cerne Abbas Giant, proudly upstanding, is viewed from a car park on the A352. The longer version of this walk assumes you saw him from there, and (while passing below his toes) explores the ancient ridgeway tracks, the chalk downland, and the old stone and hanging baskets of Cerne Abbas itself. The shorter version loses some of the ridgeway – but does offer a less foreshortened view of the chalk carving than you get from the car park.

A bridleway signpost marks a path leading up the edge of the car park, towards a farm. Before the buildings, turn right on a track, and left around a wood corner with a pond ahead. A track runs uphill between open fields.

At the track top, advance through a gap in trees to find a wide earth path running along the wooded ridge crest. Turn right on this, and follow it along the ridge of **East Hill**. After 1.5km it emerges into a narrow field. Follow the right-hand edge hedge to a field corner with a minor road just ahead.

Don't exit onto the road, but turn left around the field edge on a path for 1km, until a gate on the right leads out onto the road (signpost 'Public Site Hilfield'). Keep ahead along the road to a lay-by on the right, with a path out of the back of it. Fork left, to reach a circular car park at **Hilfield Local Nature Reserve**. There are various short waymarked trails here.

CHALK
GREENSAND

map continues
on page 156

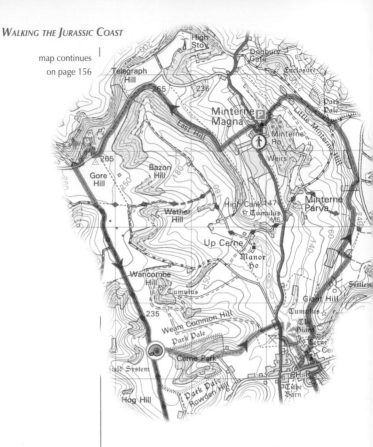

Head left out to the road, and follow it for another 200 metres to a junction. Opposite a descending side road, turn left into a sunken track, signposted as the Wessex Ridgeway. You'll be following this main ridge-line southwards for the next 6km (or 3km on the shorter route).

The track diminishes to a hedged path, which joins a track arriving from the right. Keep ahead on this, at the next junction bearing right, signed for Hog Hill, on the main track. Views on the right are of gentle chalk down-land and dry valleys.

The main track turns down right, but keep ahead on a grassy track to right of the hedge. It rises gently past a wood to a mobile phone mast. ▶

Short cut to Cerne Abbas
Below the phone mast, go through the signposted hedge gap on the left, passing the chalk block with the fossils. Head straight across a field to a wood corner, turn right on a field track, and in 50 metres take a signposted dirt

A large block of chalk on the left, placed to close a gap to tractors, has a fine display of shells and an ammonite.

CHALK FOSSILS

Inland, chalk downland generally shows no exposed rock at all – unless we count the flints that litter the fields. At the mobile phone mast on Buckland Hill, however, a 3-metre chalk boulder, placed to obstruct a hedge gap, carries the clearest chalk fossils I've seen.

Shell fossils in chalk block, Buckland Hill

The shells are of two sorts: normal bivalves (saucer shapes) and curly gastropods or sea snails. The shells themselves are gone, but their shapes are preserved as holes in the chalk, with casts of their textured outside surfaces.

The ammonite is similarly visible only as an absence. It's low down on the block on the western side. The original ring shape has been halved by the block surface, and eroded out to leave a C-shaped hole – like the handle of a teacup, but in reverse.

Early corals, along with trilobites, built their bodies out of the limestone mineral calcite: echinoderms (sea urchins etc) still do. But around 250 million years ago, nature came up with a new sort of mineral for making shells with. Aragonite, or 'mother of pearl', is a different calcium mineral used for body building by ammonites and also by the gastropods (snails). Aragonite happens to be somewhat more soluble than calcite. The chalk, which is a sort of limestone and is made of calcite, has remained stable, but the ammonites and snails within it have dissolved away.

155

track down through the wood. At the wood foot, bear slightly left, slanting around to a stile at the bottom corner of the field.

A path leads around the foot of **Weam Common Hill**, above a hedge, soon with views of the Giant. The path then leads through a wood, where you turn right on a track out to the **A352** at Larchwood care home. Turn right, to the Giant View car park.

Take the lane down towards Cerne Abbas, turning left in the lane signed for the village hall. At a stone

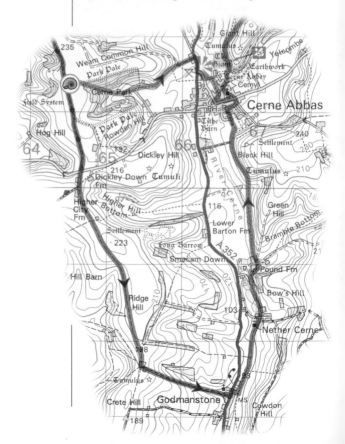

bridge (Kettle Bridge) turn right, to right of the stream. The path follows the stream into **Cerne Abbas** – ignore a left fork over a footbridge. The path leads into Mill Lane, and out to a crossroads at the New Inn. Turn left up the main street to the Giant and Royal Oak pubs, where you turn left to the church, here rejoining the main route.

From the radio mast and chalk block, continue roughly south along the ridgeline track. It crosses a lane, and continues through **Higher City Farm** opposite. Keep left, to pass to the left of a brick bungalow. The track fades to a faint grass one, still to the right of the ridge-line hedge. After 1.5km the track passes along an 'access land' meadow above Crete Bottom, an imitation ancient meadow with wildflowers.

When the track bends slightly right through a field gate, bear left through a smaller gate alongside. Continue to left of the hedge, to exit to open downland. Keep ahead, with a flint cairn up on your left. ▸ Ignore sign-posts up beyond the cairn; instead keep ahead (still south) to a gateway, and follow the hedge on your left to a signpost 100 metres ahead, named 'The Turning Point'. Here turn left, for Godmanstone. The gate leads to a grass track down field edges to Manor Farm and the A352 at the south end of **Godmanstone**. Turn left up the main road for 50 metres, then right on a footpath to a narrow footbridge beside an old mill.

The cairn is dedicated to a former walker who 'brought joy', apparently by dancing in the meadow without any clothes on...

The **small thatched building** just upstream was originally a smithy, then as the Smith's Arms, it was the smallest pub in England: its licence granted by a thirsty King Charles II. But if the future King Charles III should ever pass by, he'll find it ceased trading in 2003.

Cross a short field edge and a stile, and turn left, up-valley, to right of a hedge. A wide grass path, soon with the stream alongside it, runs up-valley, becoming a stony track as it passes above **Nether Cerne** church and manor house to reach a tarmac lane. Cross this into a hedged

River Cerne above Godmanstone

path, signed for Cerne Abbas. It passes through a wood into a field. Follow the hedge on your left, then keep on across open field, with ornamental lakes down on your left, on a faint path passing to right of a solo ash tree and then a clump of them.

At the field end a gate leads to a farm track. Keep ahead through **Pound Farm**, leaving it through wide double gates and then forking left on the track along the valley floor. The track fades at a field gate.

Cross the field to a signpost at its top right corner. Across a stile and through a scrubby patch, the path continues, wide and sometimes muddy, through small trees and bushes along the foot of the steep slope of **Black Hill**. After 800 metres, cross a stile ahead, and pass down a field to a gate to the right of allotments. The track beyond leads into **Cerne Abbas**. Keep ahead along a street called Chescombe, to be stopped against a cross-street.

You are aiming now for the church. To get there, turn right along the street for 75 metres to a tarmac path on the left. At its end, turn left in Cerne Abbas' main street to the Giant and Royal Oak pubs, where you turn right towards the church. ◀

Here the short cut route rejoins.

Cerne Abbas is said to have been founded by St Augustine, apostle to England: St Augustine's Well would be a baptismal pool, perhaps adapted from an earlier pagan site. Later the village became a staging post on this important road north: hence its many inns.

The ancientness of the chalk giant is in dispute. The earliest written reference is a bill for renovations to him in 1694 – but perhaps the people of the Middle Ages were too embarrassed to mention him? Some say he's the Roman demigod Hercules, or a Celtic equivalent. Others suggest he's a parody of Oliver Cromwell – a politician not otherwise noted for his priapic prominence.

Pass the church on your right and the manor house on your left, to a gate into the **Abbey**. Here an arch on the right leads into the Abbey graveyard. ▶ Take the left-fork path to another arch. Bear left across the field beyond, aiming for the left flank of the hill slope ahead. Pass a cattle trough to a stile into the hill-foot woods. Bear up

The right-fork path is for St Augustine's Well.

Cerne Abbas Giant

slightly right to a signpost and up wooden steps with a handrail.

The path contours around the lower slope of **Giant Hill**, passing below the Giant. ◄ The small but clear path runs above scrubby trees, then rises gently around the slope, getting a bit steeper as it rises through blackthorn shrubbery to a gate and stile at the slope top.

Paths up alongside the Giant here give no views of the Giant himself.

Cross the field ahead to a signpost at the corner of a small wood. Turn left, down the field edge to its corner, and continue down a path under trees for 50 metres to a gate on the right. A green path contours around the slope, with fences on its right and fine views.

After crossing the top of an open field, ignore a signpost up on your right but take a bridleway gate 30 metres down to its left. The path continues below fences, then through a wood, to reach a gate alongside the ridge-top road. Don't go through this gate, but turn left, slanting slightly away from the road to a small gate into a field corner.

Follow the field's left edge to a gate onto a track. Keep left along this for 500 metres, to a small gate on the left signposted for Minterne Magna. With no path, slant gradually away from the track to find a signpost standing mid-field; turn down to a small gate just below.

Minterne House, a fine Elizabethan mansion, is seen in the valley below. Its gardens are best visited in spring and early summer for magnolias and rhododendrons.

The tower and main building are in local Upper Greensand stone, with flints from the overlying chalk, and window facings in Ham Stone.

Head downhill between fields, with small gates and signposts. You join a downhill track, which fords a stream to emerge alongside **Minterne Magna** church. ◄

WALK 21
Dorsetshire Gap

Start/Finish	Woolland Hill ST 781 058 or Cheselbourne SY 764 994
Distance	25.5km (16 miles)
Ascent	550m (1800ft)
Approx time	7½hrs
Terrain	chalk escarpment and downland
Maps	Explorer 117 Cerne Abbas; Landranger 194 Dorchester
Parking	nature reserve car park on north side of Stoke Wake road just west of X-junction, also pull-off on Ibberton rd just east of the junction; lay-by at south end of Cheselbourne

'Blakemore, or Blackmoor, is a vale whose acquaintance is best made by viewing it from the summits of the hills that surround it: the bold chalk ridge that embraces the prominences of Hambledon Hill, Bulbarrow, Nettlecombe Tout, Dogbury, High Stoy and Bubb Down.

'The traveller who suddenly reaches the verge of one of these escarpments is surprised and delighted to behold, extended like a map beneath him, a country differing absolutely from that which he has passed through. Behind, the hills are open, the sun blazes down upon fields so large as to give an unenclosed character to the landscape, the lanes are white, the hedges low and plashed, the atmosphere colourless. Below, in the valley, the world seems to be constructed upon a smaller and more delicate scale; the fields are mere paddocks, so reduced that from this height their hedgerows appear a network of dark green threads overspreading the paler green of the grass. The atmosphere beneath is languorous, and is so tinged with azure that what artists call the middle distance partakes also of that hue, while the horizon beyond is of the deepest ultramarine.'

Whatever one thinks of him as a novelist, Thomas Hardy (supplying the intro for this route in *Tess of the d'Urbervilles* Chapter II) is one of England's great outdoor writers. This walk runs along that 'bold chalk ridge' from Bulbarrow to Nettlecombe Tout. Dorsetshire Gap has been a meeting of chalkland trackways for thousands of years, and hides a visitors' book for travellers of today. The southward return is through the 'colourless' chalk downs to the south.

CHALK ESCARPMENT AT BULBARROW

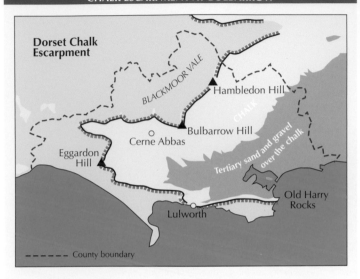

Dorset Chalk Escarpment

BLACKMOOR VALE

Hambledon Hill

CHALK

Bulbarrow Hill

Cerne Abbas

Tertiary sand and gravel over the chalk

Eggardon Hill

Old Harry Rocks

Lulworth

– – – – – County boundary

At Bulbarrow you're standing at the northern edge of Dorset's chalk escarpment. The chalk scarp stretches to left and right. Projecting below is the irregular Greensand 'bench'; it forms a plinth at the slope foot, around the 150m level, before the further drop to the stream.

In the context of Dorset, chalk counts as a tough, upstanding rock. When it and the equally tough underlying Greensand are eroded away, the land drops abruptly as mudstone and clay are uncovered underneath. The escarpment itself is roughly saucer-shaped, and northwards you look across successively older rocks underneath. The first low ground is formed of the Kimmeridge Clay (Walk 26). A few miles out, the mixed rocks of the Corallian include enough sandstone and limestone to make a definite low ridge from Hazelbury Bryan to Fifehead. The wide Blackmoor Vale beyond is eroded out of the Oxford Clay.

This walk follows the chalk escarpment west. But first, there's a drop through the Greensand onto the Kimmeridge Clay for the crossing of the Ansty gap.

Approaching Rawlsbury Camp

Head west along the road signposted for Stoke Wake, with the drop of **Bulbarrow Hill** on your right and Thomas Hardy's views north across Blackmore Vale. Keep ahead as another road joins from the left. At the next junction, keep ahead along a narrow neck of chalkland with views both ways. After 250 metres bear left through a signposted gate. ▶ A green old track runs ahead along the ridgeline to **Rawlsbury Camp** hill fort.

Follow the earthwork round to the left below the camp's summit cross to a small waymarked gate. Pass along an earthwork rampart, then down an open field with a tree strip on your right. A chalk pit is on the right as you descend to a small gate.

Chalk is porous, so we can deduce that the **ponds** in the valley to the left are on something else: they are in fact on the underlying Gault Clay at the base of the Greensand.

Head diagonally down the next field at its foot don't take the gate in the bottom corner but swerve through a gap just up to the right. A path leads down the field's left edge into hedged way.

CHALK
GREENSAND
Kimmeridge Clay

For its first 6km, the walk follows the Wessex Ridgeway, marked with distinctive 'dragon-tail' signposts

map continues on page 164

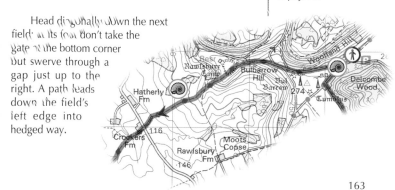

163

We are now on bare **Kimmeridge Clay** having moved down off the chalk; the ground is soggy and the path bed briefly becomes a stream. In the fields after Crockers, the path is still on the Kimmeridge Clay, but the fields are littered with cherts from the Greensand that's only recently eroded off the top.

map continues on page 166

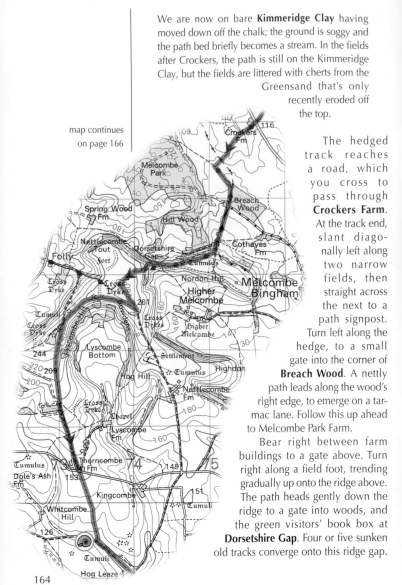

The hedged track reaches a road, which you cross to pass through **Crockers Farm**. At the track end, slant diagonally left along two narrow fields, then straight across the next to a path signpost. Turn left along the hedge, to a small gate into the corner of **Breach Wood**. A nettly path leads along the wood's right edge, to emerge on a tarmac lane. Follow this up ahead to Melcombe Park Farm.

Bear right between farm buildings to a gate above. Turn right along a field foot, trending gradually up onto the ridge above. The path heads gently down the ridge to a gate into woods, and the green visitors' book box at **Dorsetshire Gap**. Four or five sunken old tracks converge onto this ridge gap.

At the 4-way signpost bear left (for 'Folly') on an uphill path. Where it emerges to open field, keep ahead to a water tank at the downland crest. ▶

Here turn left (south), to pass through a gate and down to the right of a tree strip. There's a hidden waymark on the left at the hump of a cross dyke.

> **Cross dykes** are guardable obstructions, ditch and rampart across the ridgeline, possibly built to inconvenience prehistoric cattle raiders. Travel was always along the downland ridges in times when scrubland and bogs blocked the valley floors.

Here turn back sharp right around the rim of the south-facing **Lyscombe Bottom** to a small gate with an interpretation board. Continue around the combe rim, to take the left-hand of two gates and pass a tumulus. Head along the ridge (**Lyscombe Hill**) with the ridgeline hedge on your right.

Keep left of a wood, to head south down the rounded ridge, still with the hedge on your right. Over the hedge a large piggery is sensed rather than seen (okay, by sensed I mean smelled). A small gate leads onto its concrete access track, which is followed down to a road at **Thorncombe Farm**. Cross into a field, and head down to right of a hedge into a dry valley.

Here the walk leaves the Wessex Ridgeway.

Visitors' book, Dorsetshire Gap

Dragon signpost, Dorsetshire Gap

Porous chalk might have streams but it does have **'bottoms'**. These now dry, rounded valleys formed during the Ice Age, when the ground was perma frost, iced up all year round, and summer streams could run across the surface. They offer opportunities for low humour around place names such as Scratchy Bottom on Walk 24.

Through a small brambly gate at the field corner turn left on a path along the bottom of the 'bottom'. Bend right as valleys join, into a hedged path along the edge of **Dole's Hill Plantation**.

The original **Flintcombe Ash** in *Tess of the d'Urbervilles* was based on Dole's Ash Farm, just to the west.

'The swede-field was on the highest ground of the farm, rising above stony lanchets or lynchets—the outcrop of siliceous veins in the chalk formation, composed of myriads of loose white flints in bulbous, cusped, and phallic shapes. The whole field was in colour a desolate drab; it was a complexion without features, as if a face, from chin to brow, should be only an expanse of skin. The sky wore, in another colour, the same likeness; a white vacuity of countenance with the lineaments gone; the two girls crawling over the surface of the former like flies. The rain raced along horizontally upon the yelling wind, sticking into them like glass splinters till they were wet through.' (Chapter 43)

map continues on page 168

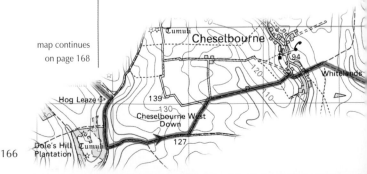

No, Thomas Hardy was not a fan of the chalk downland.

Look out for a gap on the left with inconspicuous waymarks; here cross the tiny stream, and go up with a hedge on your right, to enter a hedged green track. After rising out of the valley bear left at a junction of green tracks, to pass over the downland crest and down to a straight gravel track. Turn right along this, up and over to the road just south of **Cheselbourne**. ▸

The walk could start and finish at the parking pull-off just up the lane on the left.

Standing on chalk the small **Cheselbourne church** has no useful building stone to hand. Its builders have used as much flint as they could get away with, and stone from various quarries, to north or south, during several centuries of construction and reconstruction. Some windows are in orange Ham Stone; other crucial points at corners have white Portland Stone blocks. The roof is a mix of tile and sandstone slabs. The paler mortar is lime putty from renovations in 2014. It replaces some of the cement mortar of the 20th century, which is so inflexible that it damages the original stonework.

Note the 'scratch dial' early sundial on the left doorpost of the south porch, and two stone boys, or 'putti', from the 16th century inside the church.

Cross the lane south of the village into an uphill track. At its top bear right to a small gate. Head diagonally across a field and down into another dry valley. Follow its floor, to the left of a wood to a wall-less barn at the roadside.

Cross into a track 'unsuitable for motors' towards Dewlish Mill, but in a few steps take a gate on the left to cross a footbridge. Turn left,

This has to be the walk's sinister stretch, climbing from Devil's Brook to Gallows Corner.

upstream, and after 250 metres look out for a small gate hidden in scrub on the right. ◄ A faint path slants up scrub, through two more gates, then slants left up a field to its top corner and the start of a short fenced way. At its top a path leads ahead through a wood strip, to cross an earth track into an overgrown hedged path. This becomes a jungly tunnel to the signpost at **Gallows Corner**.

> This is more likely the site of a **gibbet**, a place where dead bodies where displayed after malefactors had been hanged at the gallows. The bodies were often placed at hilltop crossroads such as this, in chains or an iron cage, to discourage others.

Keep ahead, signed for Milton Abbas, to a crossroads named as Long Close on its signpost. Follow the road right, to **Long Close Farm**. Turn sharp left on a track up to the right-hand of two gates. Follow the left edges of two fields, then a fenced way, to emerge through a horse farm to a lane. Turn down right, keeping ahead at a junction, into **Milton Abbas**. The road bends around the corner of a lake to the foot of the thatched village street.

Milton Abbas is built to a uniform design of 'tea-cosy' cob-and-thatch cottages. The village was moved and rebuilt in 1775 as part of a Capability Brown layout of lake and grassland around the Abbey. This makes it possibly Britain's first ever housing estate.

map continues on page 170

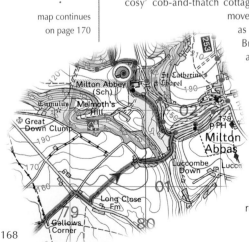

Turn left, signed for Hilton and Milton Abbey. At once bear left on a wide gravel path. It runs near the ornamental

HAM AND PORTLAND

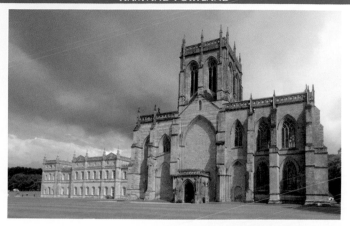

Milton Abbey House and Church (Portland Stone and Ham Stone)

At Milton Abbey the two prime building stones of Dorset stand side by side. Ham Stone and Portland Stone are both Jurassic limestones; both are 'freestone', easily worked in any direction. In the hands of a skilled mason, they both make outstandingly handsome buildings. But otherwise, they're as alike as – well – as ham, and eggs.

The abbey church is in orange Ham Stone, quarried 20 miles west in Somerset. It belongs within the Inferior Oolite that makes fine buildings from the coast up into the Cotswolds. Ham Hill itself is formed from a bank of broken shells within the Jurassic sea, and is especially uniform and easy to work. Many Dorset buildings made of their local bedrock use Ham Stone, despite the haulage costs, for tricky bits such as windows.

In striking contrast, the Abbey House alongside is in off-white Portland Stone. It's a limestone, but formed from oolites, rounded particles of calcite sand. It's less colourful, and also less carvable, than the Ham Stone alongside. The two different stones lend themselves to the different building stiles of the 15th and the 18th centuries.

The best building stone is chosen for not having any fossils to weaken it. For shells and the occasional ammonite, in either sort of stone, look at low-status sheds and field barns rather than these imposing structures.

For the geology of this fine 'inland crag' see box 'Ham and Portland'.

lake, then over a golf course to the huge **Milton Abbey** church. ◀ Turn right around its corner, then left to an urn with a car park just to the right, in front of Milton Abbey House. Exit past the small tea room to a road.

Turn left for 300 metres, then right up a wide bridleway path in woods. Past a vehicle barrier the track narrows to a path. Emerge through bracken scrub, and follow the ridge crest to a gate into a small nature reserve.

The reason why **Greenhill Down** Nature Reserve's top ground grows quite different plantlife, and even has a small pool hidden among the brambles, is because the sloping valley sides are chalk, but at the top it's covered with a layer of clay. In late spring look out for the ghostly-pale toothwort with its lilac-coloured flowers; it's a parasitic plant lacking green chlorophyll.

Continue north up the wide ridgeline, with a fence on your left, to pass Hill Barn, restored as a shelter for walkers. Join the tarmac driveway of **Bulbarrow Farm** (Dorset's highest) out to a road, with Bulbarrow's radio mast rising ahead. Turn right to a junction, with the start car park just on the left.

WALK 22
Hambledon and Hod hills

Start/Finish	The Cross, Shillingstone ST 824 113
Distance	17km (10½ miles)
Ascent	400m (1400ft)
Approx time	5hrs
Terrain	paths and tracks, small but quite steep hills
Maps	Explorers 117, 129, 118; Landranger 194 Dorchester
Parking	in Church Road, or on the A357 at the foot of a shorter footpath to the old station ST 823 115

Chalk lying on top of softer clay strata gives Hambledon and Hod hills their flat tops and steep sides. This makes for long views across the Blackmoor Vale, and also ideal strongholds in the late Stone Age, the Bronze Age and for the Romans. Chalk downland means dry and comfortable grass to walk on and wild flowers to be enjoyed. In high summer look for orchids and butterflies: in late spring it's even better, with a carpet of cowslips.

Follow Church Road (north branch, it's a U-shaped road) signed for the Parish Church. Where the lane bends, take a footpath left and pass to left of the church into a field. At its end turn right on a gravel path to the former railway

River Stour north of Shillingstone

If the station is closed you can turn right to cross the former level crossing and back left past the station.

Orchid on Hambledon Hill in July

On Hambledon Hill

line. Turn left to the station and along its refurbished platform. ◀ Cross the railway and continue on a wide path to its right, to reach the road joining Shillingstone to Child Okeford. Cross into a Trailways track, but at once fork right over a stile. A path crosses the field diagonally to back right, crosses a small footbridge, and continues along a long field to a long, high bridge over **River Stour**.

Bear half-right across the end of the field to a way-marked gate. Cross the field beyond to pass to the right of a redundant stile (ignore the field gate further left) to reach a kissing gate. The path leads along a tree avenue to a track at the edge of **Child Okeford**. Wiggle right then left onto a shady lane with houses on its right. It leads to the war memorial cross and pub at the centre of Child Okeford.

Take the road to the left of the cross, then bear right, signposted for 'Iwerne Minster'. At the edge of Child Okeford enter the driveway for Manor Barn to find the start of a field path alongside the road. At the end of the first field, rejoin the road on the left but at once turn right up a pair of parallel paths, to a kissing gate onto the base of **Hambledon Hill**.

Hambledon Hill is rich in **wildflowers** (cowslips in spring, orchids in summer) and hence in butterflies. Chalk is a form of limestone, rich in many minerals as well as calcium, but poor in nitrates, the fundamental plant nutrient. This favours low-growing and specially adapted plant life as against nitrate-greedy grass.

Head straight up onto the earthworks. The path bends right: you can follow it along the crest, or follow the top of earthworks around to the right, bending back left. Either way, reach a gate at the southeast (back left) corner. A fenced path runs past a trig point. ▶

The Neolithic earthworks here are barely visible.

The path descends gently with combes to the left and right, to a signpost above a wood. Keep ahead, along a

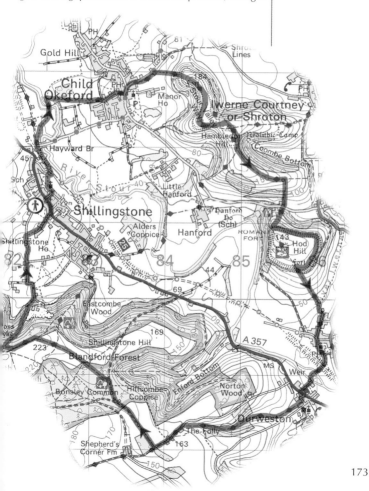

173

On Hod Hill

The difference between the Roman ramparts and the Bronze Age ones is that the Romans built with square corners.

field foot immediately above the wood, to a field gate. Continue down the rounded ridge crest, with fence on your left, for 500 metres to a tin barn. Turn down right behind this, following the field edge onto a chalky track. This runs down quite steeply to the road at Keeper's Lodge.

Cross to a gate onto the base of **Hod Hill**. A path runs directly uphill, then slants up slightly right to a gate into NT ownership. Head onto the fortifications just above. ◄ Now a path leads diagonally across (southeast) – or you can follow the rampart around to the left. In which case ignore a first gate and path down the side halfway along the eastern side.

At the fort's southeast corner, head down over a stile with gate alongside and down a hedged wide path. At the hill foot bear right along a streamside path, to head south through the edge of **Stourpaine**. Pass the church on your left, and keep ahead into a fenced field path, to reach a railway embankment.

Turn right, signposted for Durweston, under the former railway. Cross the **Stour** on a footbridge, to pass a mill pool and the mill house to A357 at **Durweston**. Turn left briefly, and cross at the war memorial into a side lane, which bends left to a track with bridleway sign on the right. After a few metres of concrete track, take the left-hand gate onto a grass track. This runs up the bottom of a dry valley into Succombe Wood (ash and beech). ▸

Where the track exits the top of the wood, keep ahead up the top end of the dry valley, to a gate beside a tiled barn conversion. It leads into a lane. Follow that ahead, past a house on either side. As it starts downhill, turn right in a wide smooth track with a patch of wood on your left.

After 750 metres the track enters **Bonsley Common Wood**. In 200 metres, after the Dorset Coppice Group Living Classroom (a hut) the track forks, both branches having vehicle barriers. Take the right-hand one, and in 300 metres bear left on a grassier track with bridleway arrows, northwest. The track exits into open fields with conservation edges (in politically correct style, sown with 'non-competitive' grasses) and runs between them past **Shillingstone Hill** trig point to a signpost at the wood edge.

Turn left along the wood edge, signed for Okeford Hill. In 250 metres bear right into the wood ('Okeford Fitzpaine'). In 100 metres, well before the outdoor centre ahead, turn down sharp right on a wide dirt track towards Shillingstone Quarry. The dirt track leads downhill, with lethal mountain bike pistes on the left and notices about the nearest A&E (Dorchester). You become aware of chalk cliffs of the quarry up right, then pass a vehicle barrier and emerge at a lane top (Lanchards Lane).

This lane leads right down into Shillingstone. However, at its foot is a short stretch of narrow busy road with bends. So after 1km, look out for a footpath on the right, with signpost and wood-earth steps to a kissing gate. The narrow nettly path runs northeast and joins the driveway of **Shillingstone House**. After 100 metres, switch to a footpath alongside the tarmac driveway, leading out to the A357 in **Shillingstone**. Turn left past a garage to the Cross.

> Waymarkers are for the Jubilee Trail.

WALK 23

Ringstead Smugglers' Path

Start/Finish	Ringstead car park SY 751 814
Distance	11.5km (7 miles); or the shorter version 5.5km (3.5 miles)
Ascent	250m (800ft); or the shorter version 150m (500ft)
Approx time	3½hrs; or the shorter version 2hrs
Terrain	shingle shore, narrow path through undercliff, very steep grass path between cliffs; cliff top path and track to return
Maps	Explorer OL15 Purbeck; Landranger 194 Dorchester
Parking	Ringstead car park

A ramble along the landslipped undercliff – with nightingales singing even in the daytime, according to the National Trust ranger – leads to the spectacular Smugglers' Path to White Nothe. This zigzags up very steep grass, and is quite exposed. Not only does it offer close ups of the chalk cliffs, with their flinty bands: it also re-enacts Chapter 10 of the Dorset thriller *Moonfleet* (J Meade Falkner, 1898).

The Zigzag started off as a fair enough chalk path, but in a few paces narrowed down till it was but a whiter thread against the grey-white cliff face, and afterwards turned sharply back, crossing a hundred feet direct above our heads... I do not believe that there were half a dozen men in England who would have ventured up that path. The ledge was little more than a foot wide, and ever so little a lean of the body would dash me on the rocks below.

Undercliff and literary zigzag make a short but very satisfying expedition. The full walk continues inland along the heights of Moigns Down.

From the car park and café the track runs seaward; but just past the toilet block, turn left on another track. It bends right, then left; in another 200 metres, and just past a house, take a stile on the right. A grass path crosses the right-hand edge of a field, then leads down steps to the beach.

White Nothe, seen ahead, has the Greensand and chalk cutting off the top of the soft Kimmeridge

White Nothe

77

Clay – a typical landslip setup. The dark colour of the clay indicates organic matter, including oily shales. These caught fire and smouldered through the 1820s, so were named Burning Cliff.

Turn left, along the beach of **Ringstead Bay**. You pass under clay cliffs and then around a headland and below a small chalk cliff, to find a ladder leading up into the undercliff level. Turn right at its top – the first few steps of the path have fallen over the cliff but after that it is clear to follow, if narrow and quite rough.

The path works its way southeastwards, through scrubby trees not far above the low cliffs at the back of the beach, and with a small pinnacle (chalk over Greensand) some distance above. Once past this point, the path slants uphill to a point below the foot of the largest cliff (chalk with flints) of the upper tier. Here it heads uphill on grass, and as the slope steepens it zigzags, heading up

White Nothe from Ringstead Bay

to right of the main cliff. Level with this cliff foot there's a terrace, but then the path zigzags upwards as steeply as before, to arrive abruptly at a marker stone on the **White Nothe** cliff top.

Turn inland past a small brick tower, to the corner of a row of houses. The cliff top path leads to the left, outside field fences. After a kissing gate, it descends on steps to another kissing gate, with a track just beyond.

Short cut avoiding Moigns Down

Cross the track onto a path that soon joins a tarmac lane. Keep ahead down this, passing a tiny church on your left, to a gate marked 'Private'. Immediately above the gate the coast path forks off left. Follow it down through scrubby woodland. After a kissing gate it becomes a wide, white track. This leads to the track junction at the toilet block alongside the car park at the walk start.

Turn right up the partly concrete track, signed for Holworth, to a T junction above a house. Turn left, and at once right, up a side track again signed for Holworth. It leads over the South Down ridgeline and downhill behind. The track becomes concrete, then a tarmac lane at **Holworth**. At the end of the houses you pass a **pond** behind the hedge on the left, to a field gate with bridleway sign.

The bridleway itself is not clear on the ground. Join a faint tractor track, just north of west and slightly uphill, passing a block of stone lying on the field. Soon you are following a fence on your left, to a small gate marked 'bull in field'. (There wasn't one when I was there.) A small path follows the fence on the left until the fence corner. Keep on ahead to join a tractor track running up to a field gate in the skyline hedge, with a small bridleway gate alongside it.

Chalk with flints above Smugglers' Path

A track runs behind the hedge, but cross it onto a fainter track half-left, running along the right-hand flank of **Moigns Down**. It fades into a field, but keep on along the ridgeline to another small gate. A small path runs along the grassland, slightly left of the ridge crest. After 1km, a grassy track slants gently down left into woodland, to emerge on the **A353** road.

Turn left on pavement, down around a bend where you ignore a first lane down to the left. In another 300 metres, take the lane down left signed for Ringstead and which you must (unless born and raised at Ringstead itself) have used to drive to the walk start. Follow it for 800 metres down through **Upton** and up to a bend to the left.

Take the stile ahead, signposted for Spring Bottom. Go through two gates and head directly uphill, a hedge to your left. At the top a stile leads to a path descending through woodland, ornamented with artificial pools in the stream to your right.

Cross a stile at the slope foot, bending left to a complex path junction. Don't ford the stream ahead, or cross the wooden footbridge immediately downstream, but turn left on a wide path signed 'Ringstead' over another stile. Immediately turn right, on a narrow, overgrown path, which at once crosses the stream on a wider, concrete bridge. The path contours due south within a narrow strip of woodland, then descends to cross a field track and meet the Coast Path immediately below.

Turn left, following the path through scrubby woodland. It dips to cross a stream, and here a side path leads down to the shingle beach nearby. But keep ahead, soon joining a gravel track past beach houses. The track bends left, to a track junction just before the toilet block and the car park with café at **Ringstead**.

LULWORTH COVE

Lulworth Cove

Lulworth walks two ways. Westwards (Walk 24) are tremendous chalk cliffs, and the UK coastline's most photographed feature at Durdle Door. Eastwards (Walk 25) is the Fossil Forest. Add to this Lulworth itself, where the Purbeck/Portland beds are splendidly squashed up at Stair Hole, or stand erect in seastacks and corners of the cliff; meanwhile the Greensand, companion since Peak Hill over 50 miles of coastline, comes down to beach level to be inspected for its seashells.

At the end of Walk 24, you can walk straight through the car park and into Walk 25, for a 5½hr combination walk of chalk, limestone, Greensand, and great, grassy clifftops.

WALK 24
Lulworth Cove and Coast

Start/Finish	Lulworth Bay Heritage Centre SY 822 800
Distance	10.5km (6½ miles)
Ascent	400m (1400ft)
Approx time	3½hrs
Terrain	good coastal path, grassy chalk ridges; the return from West Bay is strenuous with steep ups and downs
Maps	Explorer OL15 Purbeck; Landranger 194 Dorchester
Parking	huge car park at Lulworth Cove

Chalk cliffs west of the village, and then Durdle Door and Stair Hole. Regrettably, Lulworth's great geology stands above and around several fine beaches and makes up 8km of spectacular coastal scenery – so there are long queues for fish and chips, and you have to politely ask people to take their damp swimwear off the Greensand/Chalk boundary. Okay, so we don't really mind the beaches and the scenery. But they're even more enjoyable outside the peak holiday season.

CHALK
GREENSAND
WEALDEN clay
PURBECK
PORTLAND

Leave the car park by the gate at its top end, but at once turn to the right off the big, wide main path. A path through scrubby bushes leads around the toe of **Hambury Tout**, then bends left up the quiet dry valley hidden behind it. It follows the foot of fields to reach a track near the 'Durdle Door' car park up above **St Oswald's Bay**.

Turn right, up past caravans, to **Newlands Farm**. The road from West Lulworth is just above, but turn left between the farm buildings onto an enclosed track running west. It emerges to a field above the hollow of Scratchy Bottom.

Pass along the rim of the hollow, staying below a hedge of gorse bushes to its corner. An interpretation board is just above, around the hedge corner. But the path (very faint) keeps straight ahead, passing to right of a **tumulus**, to a gate with signpost.

Now you follow the top edges of fields, straight ahead along the chalk ridgeline, with the sea far below you. After 1.5km you pass well left of a pointed obelisk, the upper of two mile markers for shipping. Some stone bays are by the path, two with sculptures in. Straight after this the ridgeline dips to a slight col. Here stay to the left of a fence, as it bends left and slants downhill to join the Coastal Path.

Turn sharp left, as the Coastal Path runs gently down around the top of the West Bottom hollow. Then it steepens down past the lower of the two mile markers. The path drops to a dip, Middle Bottom, then rises on an inland-facing slope just below the cliff edge, to the top of **the Warren**. The path drops again, to a dip above a bay with a sea stack at the west end and the natural arch Bat's Hole through the headland below the Warren.

The chalk of **Bat's Head** and the sea stack, the **Butter Rock**, have both been tilted upright by the Alpine earth movements. You can tell because the flint bands, instead of being horizontal, run

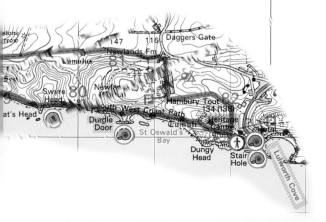

Butter Rock sea stack, west of Lulworth

From here you should see a tiny hole right through the top edge of the rock above the arch. It was left by a fossil treetrunk – see 'Fossil Forest' box in Walk 25.

directly up and down. Looking down on the Butter Rock, you see reefs where two other stacks have been chopped off by the waves.

The path rises over **Swyre Head**, and drops to Scratchy Bottom, the dip above the bay of Durdle Door. Continue along the cliff top to the interpretation board above **Durdle Door** sea arch. ◀ Here paths lead down to both Durdle Door Bay and the next one east, Man o' War Bay.

The back of **Durdle Door Bay** is often ignored in favour of the spectacular Durdle Door in front. But here there's the junction, tilted almost vertical, of the Greensand (pale yellow rather than green, with shelly fossils) and the chalk. Further west, the Alpine earth movements have broken the chalk apart and shoved it past itself along a horizontal fault plane (a 'thrust'). The sea has exploited the shattered fault-line rocks to carve a row of little caves. Between them, you see the fault plane itself, turned yellow by the heat and pressure of the moving earth.

Continue along the cliff top path above Man o' War Bay to a fork. Here the coast path has been swept away by a cliff fall above **St Oswald's Bay** (May 2013) so follow diversion signs up the left-fork path, wide and dusty. At the slope top, a grass path bears right, contouring to rejoin the cliff top beyond the landslip. The path ahead slants down the steep face of Hambury Tout, wide and with stone steps, to the gate back into the **Lulworth Ray** car park ▸

Thrust fault in chalk, Durdle Door Bay

Continue on Walk 25 or at least visit Stair Hole at the start W N.

THE DURDLE WALL: PORTLAND AND PURBECK ERECT

The Lulworth Crumple

Most of the Jurassic Coast lies comfortably flat, with the Greensand at around the 100m mark all the way from High Peak (Sidmouth) to White Nothe just west of here. But the Lulworth corner of the coast has been hit by interesting distant disasters: the long, slow crunch of Africa into Europe, and the shoving up of the Alps at the northern end of Italy. Like a ruckle moving across a carpet, the far-away mountain building has raised this corner of England.

Two beds in particular stand upright all along this walk. The Portland and Purbeck Stones, only 30 metres thick even when added together, make a series of special sea features. A line of reefs off Swyre Head (the Calf, the Cow, the Blind Cow, the Bull) suddenly becomes the upright arched wall of Durdle Door. The Portland and Purbeck come ashore again west of Lulworth, where the Alpine mountain-building happens almost before your eyes as the Lulworth Crumple at Stair Hole.

At Lulworth Cove, the sea has broken through the Purbeck/Portland band, and is energetically hollowing out the softer Wealden Clay behind, as well as the Greensand and chalk at the bay's back. The same happens at the combined Mupe Bay and Worbarrow Bay on Walk 25. The entrance corners, Mupe Rocks and the tilted fang of Worbarrow Tout, are formed from the Purbeck and Portland Stones.

WALK 25
Lulworth Cove and the Fossil Forest

Start/Finish	Lulworth Bay Heritage Centre SY 822 800
Distance	6km (3¾miles)
Ascent	250m (800ft)
Approx time	2hrs
Terrain	Good coastal path, grassy chalk ridges; one steep ascent
Maps	Explorer OL15 Purbeck; Landranger 194 Dorchester
Parking	huge car park at Lulworth Cove
Note	Lulworth Ranges are open most weekends, over Christmas, and during school summer holidays, but otherwise closed; check at www.dorsetcoast.com (Resources)

Just inside the Lulworth Ranges is the Fossil Forest, the outline of trees embalmed in algal slime and preserved in Purbeck Limestone. (The steps down to its ledge were closed due to a small landslip in 2015, but are due to reopen Autumn 2019.) Continue to Mupe Bay, a cirque of chalk standing above brown and orange Wealden Clay and rocky arms of the Portland/Purbeck beds. All this converts in walking terms to a good coast path, a stiff chalky zigzag, and a gentle ridgeline back to Lulworth Cove.

At the foot of the car park, pass to the right behind the **Heritage Centre** on a path up to **Stair Hole**. ▶ The path continues to a tall inscribed stone (marking the World Heritage Site) above Lulworth Cove. Turn left, down to the bay (café here).

If the tide is fully in, you may have to take the coast path. This heads up behind the café, then contours left to avoid a cliff fall (2014). After joining B3070 for 400m past a row of cottages, it turns up to the right, and contours back to pass around the head of the bay at cliff top level. Otherwise it's better to cross the beach below, saving 120m of ascent and getting a look at the Greensand/chalk boundary and some fossilised tree bits (black carbonated

See 'Durdle Wall' box in Walk 24.

CHALK
GREENSAND
WEALDEN clay
PURBECK
PORTLAND

Fossil soil layer (palaeosol) at the fossil forest, Lulworth Cove

fragments called lignite) in the Wealden Clay. Pass along the shingle to the bay's easternmost point, where a wooden ladder mounts to the top of the low cliff. Head inland for 100 metres to a path junction with a marker stone, where you turn right through scrubby woods to emerge above the sea near the cove's eastern corner.

Turn left, to the gate through the tall fence around the Lulworth Ranges. ◄ Through the gate, bear down right to the steps leading down to the cliff ledge with the Fossil Forest. (Or, sometimes, don't – in 2015 the cliff collapsed onto these steps.)

Occasionally red flags fly when they shouldn't: there's a timetable on the gate, and if the gate is open, then the ranges are open.

Return up the steps, and turn right along the cliff tops. In 1km you arrive at the corner of Brandy Hole, and having rounded this small bay, you reach the corner of **Mupe Bay**. Steps lead down to the beach here.

FOSSIL FOREST

The Portland Stone formed as sandbanks under a warm, shallow sea through which giant ammonites squirted themselves on jets of water. Over the next 5 million years the sea level fell, and the ground became a shoreline swamp, where large conifer trees grew out of a smelly algal slime called stromatolite.

The trees died and rotted away. But the stromatolite contained a gritty skeleton of the limestone mineral calcite. That calcite formed rock, preserving the lumpy shapes of the stromatolite but also the outlines of the trees that stood or fell over into the slime. Some remnants of the trees themselves (pickled in silica mineral) were also preserved over 139,999,950 years, but were then removed by collectors. However, you can see fossils of these actual trees, a precursor of the cypress, at the Heights Hotel on Portland and the Portland Museum.

Below the stromatolite is a dark, pebbly layer: these Dirt Beds are the actual soil that the trees were rooted in. In the back wall of the ledge is a more brittle limestone, which has yielded to the Alpine earth movements by shattering apart: the Broken Beds. And above all the layers is an interpretation board that carries this important educational message: 'don't believe everything on interpretation boards'! (If you miss the message, see the photo and caption at the end of this walk.)

Mupe Bay is a good place to look at the **Wealden Clay**. The strata hereabouts are upright, with younger rocks inland. The back of the combined Mupe-Worbarrow Bay is tall chalk; the corners next to the sea are Purbeck and Portland Limestone beds. In between, the bay has been hollowed into the Wealden Clay, seen alongside the beach steps, and in the east side of Worbarrow Bay opposite.

The clay, 700m deep, is the bed of a great freshwater lake that stretched eastwards to the Weald itself in Kent, eventually to be overwhelmed by the

A lesson in not believing interpretation boards at Lulworth's Fossil Forest. Mischievously, the dinosaurs on the lower panel are being hunted by an early caveman. Humans would not arrive for another 139 million years. Also the trees are shown as palms rather than conifers.

incoming Cretaceous sea. Its lively yellow, grey and pinkish colours are caused by the amount of iron, and whether that iron has remained oxidised (rusty) in clear water, or has been chemically reduced to grey in stagnant water with dead plants in.

The path heads around the bay, then zigzags very steeply up **Bindon Hill**. At the slope top turn left, with a fence on your right, along the ridge of Bindon Hill. The path leads past a radar station to a gate out of Lulworth Ranges. Through this, turn left, following the range fence down off the ridge. As the slope steepens, the path turns right, along the top edge of scrubby woods overhanging Lulworth Cove. At the corner of the bay, the direct path down left has been carried away by a cliff fall. The path ahead contours away from the cliff top, then after 300m drops left to join the B3070, the road leading down to the Heritage Centre.

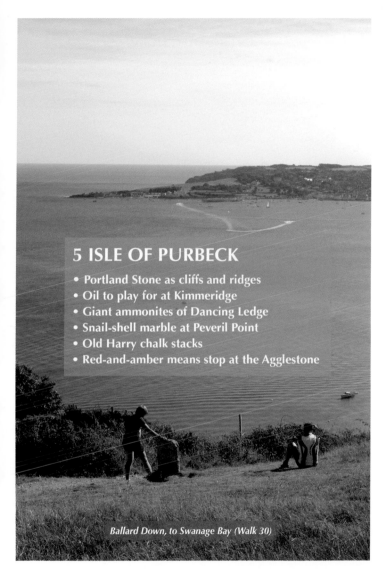

5 ISLE OF PURBECK

- Portland Stone as cliffs and ridges
- Oil to play for at Kimmeridge
- Giant ammonites of Dancing Ledge
- Snail-shell marble at Peveril Point
- Old Harry chalk stacks
- Red-and-amber means stop at the Agglestone

Ballard Down, to Swanage Bay (Walk 30)

INTRODUCTION

Expansion cracks in dolomite stone, Kimmeridge Bay (Walks 26 and 27)

At the top of the Jurassic come two thick and chunky layers of limestone. The Portland Stone and the overlying Purbeck Beds are pale creamy yellow, and solid enough to stand out in spectacular landscape. They're both full of fossil interest, with the Portland's big ammonites and the Purbeck's fossil trees.

The Portland-Purbeck slab formed fine sea features all the way along from Portland itself, including Durdle Door and the Lulworth Crumple in the previous section. Behind Kimmeridge Bay, this tough slab heads inland,

as the ridgeline to Swyre Head. Meanwhile the sea cliffs below take on the one colour that the Jurassic Coast hasn't yet been seen in: the classic black of the Kimmeridge Clay.

But then the pale Portland Stone comes back to the seaside. Now lying roughly flat, it forms the high cliffs of Houns Tout, then descends to sea-cliff level at St Aldhelm's Head. And from here to Swanage, the sea scenery is simple: Portland Stone (with the occasional sea-washed ammonite) and broken looking Purbeck Beds on top.

WALK 26

Kimmeridge, Tyneham and Flower's Barrow

Start/Finish	Kimmeridge SY 918 800
Distance	14km (9 miles); or short cut at Tyneham Goyle 11.5km (7 miles) or Tyneham Cap 8.5km (5 miles)
Ascent	450m (1500ft); or short cut at Tyneham Goyle 300m (1000ft) or Tyneham Cap 150m (500ft)
Approx time	4½hrs; or short cut at Tyneham Goyle 3½hrs or Tyneham Cap 2½hrs
Terrain	wide, waymarked paths through the Lulworth Ranges
Maps	Explorer OL15 Purbeck; Landranger 195 Bournemouth
Parking	car park in quarry (Portland Stone) above Kimmeridge village; also at Kimmeridge Bay, reached via toll road
Note	Lulworth Ranges are open most weekends, over Christmas, and during school summer holidays, but otherwise closed; check at www.dorsetcoast.com (Resources)

Steep-sided downland ridges – the mile over Tyneham Cap could be the best bit of ridge in all Dorset – ring the abandoned village at Tyneham. They're almost like the ramparts of Flowers' Barrow, on a greatly enlarged scale... Chalk-backed Mupe Bay is impressive, and being a good 15 minutes' walk from the car park is less busy than many on the south coast, with the firepower of the British Army's tanks assuring no caravan parks at all.

For rock interest, there are tree bits in the clay cliffs of Worbarrow Bay, the impressive Purbeck-Portland lump of Worbarrow Tout and oil field geology in the dusky coloured cliffs of Kimmeridge. To all this add, at walk's end, the fine new Etches fossil museum.

Turn right (west) out of the car park and cross a road junction, passing a stile on the left to a gate with a sign about whether the Range Paths ahead are open. Pass along a field foot, above a fence and the steeper slope dropping to the sea – fine views here. A second field leads to a kissing gate at the flagpole into Lulworth Ranges.

CHALK
GREENSAND
WEALDEN clay
PURBECK
PORTLAND

On Tyneham Cap, heading to Kimmeridge Bay

A track slants down left – it's the Range Path to Kimmeridge oil well – but keep ahead on a lesser, grassy track following the ridgeline. Both these tracks, like all of the walks through Lulworth Ranges, have little yellow marker posts on both sides.

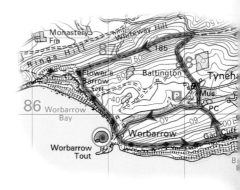

The grassy track runs along the ridgeline, with great views both ways. After 1.5km, the track descends to a path junction on the slope of **Tynham Cap** across a cattle grid. Here note a yellow-post-marked path that turns down sharp left to run just below a broken wall. This path will be the return route of the walk to Kimmeridge Bay. ▶

Take it now for the shortest version of this walk.

Continue ahead on the track along the ridge crest: the imposing overhang of **Gad Cliff** is ahead. The path moves onto the inland flank of this. Just before a stile, a milestone-type marker indicates the range path turning down to the right for Tyneham. It heads down the fence to a stile and gate just below, and takes a track zigzagging downhill to a gate and stile near Tyneham Farm (which has toliets, and a history presentation in the barn).

Short cut: Tynham Goyle

Just below this gate near Tyneham Farm, turn left on a stony well used track down Tyneham Gwyle (Goyle). ▶ Where the track divides, take the wide path shortcutting a slight bend, rejoining past a ruined cottage.

'Goyle' is a wooded stream hollow. Woods here contain shrapnel and so won't ever be chainsawed down.

The track arrives at the corner of **Worbarrow Bay**, itself part of the wide Mupe Bay. A few metres past the flagpole, steps on the left lead up past a stone wall to a picnic table and the kissing gate of the Coast Path up Gold Down. Continue on the main route (see below).

Below the gate near Tyneham Farm, take the track ahead, across the valley. It passes car parks to the former post office of the abandoned **Tyneham village**, whose population was evicted at the start of World War Two to let the area become a military training range.

Past the Post Office bear up slightly left. Pass to the left of the church (or through it, if open, as it usually is), to a kissing gate just above. The white, stony track above slants up left, then back up to the right to the crest of **Whiteway Hill**. Just before reaching the tarmac road along the ridge, turn left on a stony track. This follows the ridge crest west, passing a trig point. The track turns away downhill but a path leads forward through a gap in the earthworks of **Flower's Barrow**. An interpretation board and picnic table are in the hollow within the ramparts.

> **Flower's Barrow** makes a change from the small Bronze Age barrows that abound around here. This much bigger one belongs to the more populated and aggressive Iron Age. Its ramparts were for defence against neighbouring tribes, its hut circles inhabited by the Durotriges, whose capital was at Maiden (Mai Dun) Castle near Dorchester and who gave Dorset its name.
>
> The fort's ridgeline position was even more commanding then, when wetter climate meant soggy valleys and only the ridgelines passable. About half of the hill fort has been carried away by 2000 years of cliff erosion.

Once inside the earthwork, turn back to the left, descending through a kissing gate. The path descends, very steeply to start with, to the left of the cliff top fence, right down to sea level again, to cross a footbridge where the Tynham stream flows into **Worbarrow Bay**. ◀

Head up a track for a few metres, before turning right up steps to low stone ruins and a picnic table. ◀ A gate leads onto the ridge end of Gold Down, with a path to the left of the crest along **Gad Cliff**.

Fossil timber bits are found in the clay cliffs.

The Tynham Goyle short-cut rejoins here.

MUPE BAY AND WEALDEN CLAY

Lulworth Cove and Mupe Bay are a simple result of soft and hard rock layers. Between the hard Purbeck/Portland Limestones below, and the fairly hard chalk layers above, the Wealden Beds are a 400-metre thickness of river clay. The rock layers have been pushed up vertical, so that the sequence coming in from the sea is limestone –

Fossil timber, Mupe Bay

Wealden Clay – chalk. Once the sea has broken a gap in the limestone, it can carve a deep bay into the Wealden before coming up against the chalk.

Swanage Bay is formed in the same Wealden Clay, but this time the sea has come in sideways, from the east. An inland valley, between the Chalk ridge (north) and the Purbeck one (south) connects Mupe Bay and Swanage Bay. The Weald itself, from Essex to Hampshire, is where the chalk layer originally folded into a long ridge. The highest, central part has eroded away to expose the softer clays, while the remaining chalk forms the North and South Downs.

Being inland (lake bed) sediment, the Wealden Clay contains trees. Quite unlike the fossil trees of Lulworth, fossil timber at Worbarrow Bay forms black coal-like streaks within the clay. Larger fragments appear like the lumps of cracked, charred timber found in the embers of a bonfire. Fossil timber can be seen in the first few metres of the low clay cliffs in Worbarrow Bay west of the track foot.

As the path passes above Tynham village, it becomes a wide green track along a rounded crest, rejoining the outward route to the path junction on Tyneham Cap. With the gate and cattle grid just ahead, this time you fork down right between yellow marker posts to a path junction with a shelter seat. Here keep down to the right at a marker stone. The path slants downhill around the steep face of **Tyneham Cap** above Brandy Bay, with a zig-zag back to the right to rejoin the cliff top below. Keep on down field edges alongside the cliff top, to a field corner at the **Broad Bench headland**. ▸ Here turn sharp left, to a cattle grid and a smooth gravel track.

All around the headland is a classic example of a wave-cut platform.

Kimmeridge Bay (black Kimmeridge Clay)
and Gad Cliff (Portland Stone) behind

Access to the beach
is down to the right
here; geology info
box at Walk 27.

The track runs above the sea, after 600 metres leaving the Lulworth Ranges. Keep ahead past the 'nodding donkey' oil well at **Kimmeridge Bay**. Where the track bends left at houses take the path ahead, dipping to cross a stream. ◄ The path ascends to the corner of a car park.

Turn left along the car park edge, inland, to a lane. Follow it ahead across a small stream to a stile and gate on the right. A path runs along field edges next to the stream for 800 metres. As it enters a small wood, the path divides, each branch crossing the stream. Turn right over the right-hand footbridge, and follow the left edge of a field to a stile and the road just beyond.

Café and the
magnificent
Etches Collection
fossil museum.

Head up through **Kimmeridge**. ◄ Where the road bends right, keep ahead up steps, to pass to the right of the church on a stone path to a small gate. Head straight up the field above to a stile and a road junction, with the walk start car park immediately to the right.

WALK 27

Swyre Head and Houns Tout

Start/Finish	Kimmeridge shore SY 908 791
Distance	14km (8½ miles); or shorter version 8km (5 miles)
Ascent	350m (1100ft); or shorter version 250m (800ft)
Approx time	4¼hrs; or shorter version 2½hrs
Terrain	grassy tracks and paths; high inland ridge, then coast path
Maps	Explorer OL15 Purbeck; Landranger 195 Bournemouth
Parking	Shore parking down toll road from Kimmeridge village; also quarry at lane junction above Kimmeridge SY 918 800; and, on longer route, west of Kingston SY 943 792 and SY 953 794

Swyre Head feels like a sea cliff; and probably was one, at times of higher sea level during the ice ages. It's a continuation of the Portland Stone that provided actual cliff tops around Portland itself and will do so again at St Aldhelm's Head.

The return is along present-day sea cliffs a couple of kilometres further south. They're of grey clay and bituminous shale, so quite unlike the Portland cliffs that once stood above a sea full of ice floes. The Portland former cliffs are grassed over; the Kimmeridgean current ones are only seen from above on their cliff top path. So the walk is fossil free, more energetic than intellectual. Kimmeridge Bay itself, however, demands a wander over the fossil ledges below its sombre black cliffs.

A path runs along the field edges to the left of the stream for 800 metres. At the edge of a small wood, the path divides, each branch crossing the stream. Turn right over the first of the footbridges, and follow the left edge of a field to a stile and the road just beyond.

Head up through **Kimmeridge**, passing between the new Etches Collection fossil museum (opened in 2017) and a farm café. Where the road bends right, keep ahead up steps to pass to the right of the church to a small gate.

PORTLAND
Kimmeridge Clay

MAKING CLAY AT KIMMERIDGE BAY

There are two sorts of rock ledges reaching into Kimmeridge Bay. The dark-coloured, seaweedy ones are the place to find ammonites, nicely displayed in white aragonite (their original shell mineral) against the black stone. The yellowish, seaweed free ledges continue up in the cliffs as hard, pale orange bands within the dark Kimmeridge Clay. They look like sedimentary lime-stone beds: but they aren't.

Rock formation, at around 2km underground, is quite a bit more compli-cated than patting together a sand castle with a spade. Heat and pressure in the dark shales mean that bacteria and other organic matter are sweated out as oil. The Kimmeridge shales are the source rock of North Sea oil, and lumps of the shale can, with difficulty, be set alight to smoulder black smoke. (The 'nodding donkey' oil well at the western end of the bay is, however, harvest-ing from a quite different rock band, the Cornbrash, here buried 550m deep.)

Most ammonites land flat on the sea bed. But the odd one that landed on the edge now shows the crushing effect of the rock formation, com-pressed to as little as 10 per cent of its original thickness.

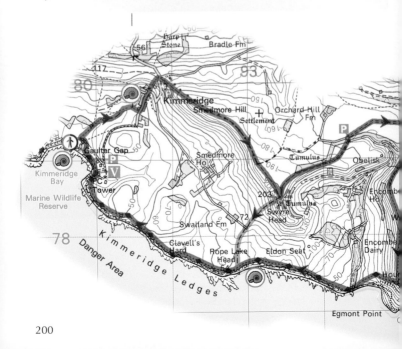

Meanwhile, those hard, pale orange layers that look like limestone but aren't? The lack of fossils in them is a clue. Their dolomite mineral is chemically close to limestone but formed quite differently: not as sediment layers but by self-assembly in the heat and pressure 2km underground. The Washing Ledge sticks into the sea below the cliff top cottages, and runs on west-

Washing Ledge dolomite band, Kimmeridge Bay

wards climbing up within the cliff. It's a strangely symmetrical sandwich, with a central dark band of shale; the dolomite has lumped and crystallised itself equally on either side of this central band.

The dolomite platform further west, alongside the warning sign for the Lulworth Ranges, shows an even odder effect of the rock's underground self-assembly. The dolomite mineral takes up more space than the mixed material it came from, so it formed in a compressed state. Once exposed by erosion it expands, in overlapping plates several metres wide. The edges of these 'mega-polygons' are raised 20cm or so above the surrounding rock, and you can see the scratched surfaces where the edge of one polygon has crept over another.

Head straight up the field above to a stile and a road junction. ▶

Kimmeridge Bay is best explored at low tide, which could be either the start or the end of the walk. It's reached from the main car park's western corner, by a stepped path down into a stream hollow. The walk starts northwest along the continuation of the car park lane, across a small stream to a stile and gate on the right.

Keep ahead on the uphill road for 100 metres, then turn right up a wide, stony track. It runs along the crest of **Smedmore Hill**. After 1.5km, where the track bends left, take a small gate ahead, marked as Heaven's Gate. The path continues along the crest, to the left of a wall, to the trig point on **Swyre Head**.

The quarry car park, one of three car parks en route serving as possible start/finish points, is just to the right.

Swyre Head has received particular attention from peak-baggers, who in 2002 ruled that the Stone Age tumulus had now been there long enough to become an integral part of the hill. Raising the hill to 208m, this gives it the 150m drop to qualify for 'Marilyn' hill list status.

Short cut to coast path

A permissive path descends directly to Rope Lake Head. You miss the high cliff top of Houns Tout, but get more time for the ammonites back at Kimmeridge.

The path starts at a stile midway between Swyre Head's trig point and the tumulus that forms its actual summit. The path zigzags down the steep (Portland Stone) scarp to a gate at the top corner of a field. Through this, go down with a fence to your left, to another stile. Turn briefly left, then down through a gate on a path that soon joins a farm track.

Where the track bends right towards **Swalland Farm**, keep ahead down the right-hand edge of a field, to a stile onto the coastal path. On the left are the white-striped cliffs described below. Turn right on the coastal path continuing over **Rope Lake Head** and along the cliff tops to **Kimmeridge**.

In front of **Swyre Head's** summit tumulus turn back sharp left (north) to continue along the brink of the drops above Encombe. Pass alongside Polar Wood to a gate. A faint track continues ahead into the field, leaving the scarp edge. Midfield the track bends slightly left, to a tree strip. Ignore a track to the right, and keep ahead between ornamental stone gate posts to Sheep Pens Car Park on the lane west of Kingston.

Turn right, along the lane, towards Kingston – on the way there's a view north to Corfe Castle. The lane reaches woods, with another car park. Just after this (and before reaching **Kingston**) turn back sharp right on a wide, smooth track signed for Houns Tout. The track emerges at the top of a grass escarpment looking back west to Swyre Head. Follow the scarp top south, with a wall on your

left, to the point where it becomes an actual sea cliff at the top of **Houns-tout Cliff**.

Here (before you reach a stone bench) the Coastal Path turns down sharp right. And now you simply follow the tops of sea cliffs westwards. At the first dip, above Egmont Bight, there's no longer access to the shore as Freshwater Steps have been removed by the sea. The Coast Path rises over Eldon Seat and dips to a footbridge marked as having been moved 20 metres inland due to coastal erosion. The path then rises to **Rope Lake Head**.

> Back to the east, the cliffs are striped with **coccolith limestone**; the off-white bands are essentially the same stuff as chalk. A late-Jurassic geologist would never have suspected that this odd off-colour band was about to become the only rock there was, piling up hundreds of metres thick.

The cliff top path rises to the cliff top called Cuddle, then dips to pass Clavell Tower. ▶ Steps lead down to the corner of **Kimmeridge Bay** at the Marine Reserve Centre. You can descend to the foreshore here, to pass over the shale and dolomite ledges to the beach path alongside the car park.

Cliff east of Rope Lake Head, view to Houns Tout and St Aldhelm's Head

This folly has been moved 35 metres inland to save it from cliff erosion.

WALK 28
Chapman's Pool and St Aldhelm's Head

Start/Finish	Worth Matravers north edge SY 973 776
Distance	9.5km (6 miles); or shorter version 6km (3½ miles)
Ascent	300m (1000ft); or shorter version 150m (500ft)
Approx time	3hrs; or shorter version 2hrs
Terrain	paths, some quite steep and slippery; wooded hollow and grassy cliff tops
Maps	Explorer OL15 Purbeck; Landranger 195 Bournemouth
Parking	pay and display Worth Matravers north edge; also west of the village SY 964 774

Chapman's Pool has been praised as one of Dorset's best quiet beaches. To some it is unsettling, with its great cliffs of unstable grey mud. But being free of convenient car parks, it is certainly quiet. The approach is by hidden stream valleys, or 'bottoms', sunken into the softer Portland Sands below the plateau of Purbeck and Portland Stone. The atmosphere is again more weird than pretty.

To preserve the mental unease caused by uncanny landscape, cut short the walk and head straight back to Worth Matravers to explore the fossils and cramped corridors of the Square & Compass. Otherwise, any Chapman's Pool disquiet is well blown away on the full-length version of the walk, an airy cliff top circuit around St Aldhelm's Head.

PURBECK
PORTLAND
Kimmeridge Clay

Head south into the village for 75 metres, but before the Square and Compass pub turn right onto a small path between houses. Turn left along the backs of the houses, to a field corner with signpost.

Turn right ('Hill Bottom'), up the field edge, across a gentle ridgeline, and down the edge of the following field. In its corner is a stone stile over a broken wall. Across this, the path heads down into a gradually deepening valley. It becomes a wooded, enclosed hollow or 'bottom'.

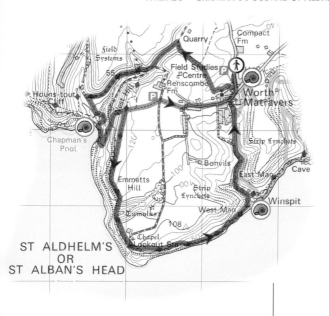

ST ALDHELM'S
OR
ST ALBAN'S HEAD

At its foot the hollow runs into another one, Hill Bottom. Turn left down this, to join a tarmac lane at its foot. As the valley opens out, keep to right of the stream up to a group of houses. Above Hill Bottom Cottage turn left, on a green track that contours around the base of a wooded spur, soon with Chapman's Pool down on its left.

On the point of the spur, the green track reaches the start of a tarmac lane. Here turn left, away from the tarmac, straight down the field to a stile. Across it turn left briefly, then head down steps to an underwater footbridge. A muddy path leads downstream to **Chapman's Pool**. ▶

Head left around the foreshore – at high tide this is threatened by unstable mud cliffs; keep out from the foot of them. Just after boat houses, turn inland up a wide, well-surfaced path (a former track to the boathouses). This bends back left to northwards, under landslipped

Note that the bridleway path from here up to West Hill has been carried away by a mudslide.

CHAPMAN'S POOL

The black shale slabs in the beach show many ammonites. These predatory seashells fell to the stagnant sea floor from more oxygenated layers above – the ones that landed on the edge have been crushed down flat by the process of rock formation. Oysters that lived in the sludgy depths found the dead ammonites useful anchor points, so you sometimes see the two fossils squashed together.

Ammonite and oyster, Chapman's Pool

The foreshore boulders are of several different sorts. As well as the black shaly mudstone with the ammonites, there are yellowish blocks of cherty Portland Stone, as seen now at the very top of Houns-tout. There is also dark dolomite stone (see Walk 27); occasionally this has crystals of a black form of calcite. The Massive Bed, from half-way up Houns-tout, is blue-grey in the centre but yellow-brown where outer layers have been exposed to the air; it has fossil shrimp burrows.

Chapman's Pool and Houns Tout

cliffs. A rough path crosses the landslipped area, to join the track beyond.

After a gate, continue 100 metres, until a path with waymark post and wooden handrail forks up to the right. It zigzags up steep **West Hill** to its flat top, where there's a path junction with marker stone.

Short cut back to Worth Matravers

Here you could head directly back to Worth Matravers. Cross the stile ahead and head inland on a well used path across two fields to the end of a car park. Cross the car park foot and a track beyond to a small gate. Head along to right of a hedge to Weston Farm. Pass out to the left of the buildings to a lane, where you keep ahead to **Worth Matravers**.

Turn right along the cliff top path. After 1.5km it passes a memorial garden to Royal Marines. It continues along the gently level top of the Portland Stone; then suddenly it doesn't, at an incised valley. ▶ This means a steep stepped descent and climb back up again, to **St Aldhelm's Head** with its coastguard station.

As you pass around the cliff top **St Aldhelm's Chapel** is over on your left. ▶ You then pass a memorial sculpture above a wartime radar station.

In another 200 metres or so, turn right alongside a fence descending towards the sea, to find the path again

Houns-tout from St Adhelm's coast path

The Portland Stone is a slab 30 metres thick, and a post-Ice Age stream has cut down into the soft Portland Sands underneath.

The chapel predates the Portland Stone quarries here, and is made of the overlying Purbeck Stone.

at a slightly lower level. It slants down across a fairly steep slope, and is uncomfortably slippery after rain with a sticky clay-and-lime mud that builds up under your feet.

The path reaches the sea shore and follows it to the quarry at **Winspit**. Here it heads up left around the quarry rim, to join a track. You'll be heading inland along this: but first, turn down right to poke around in the old quarry. ◄

> **Winspit Quarry** was dug into the upper layers of the Portland Stone. The cave entrances have been fenced against humans, while still letting in the bats. Chert lumps are scattered through the limestone. Here and there you'll spot a pair of twin holes, like staring eyes. The two holes connect inside the rock: they're the eroded out cast of half an ammonite.
>
> Where the track reaches the sea, the left-hand rock wall has the underlying Portland Cherty Series (really cherty and so not quarried), and you might spot a sea-washed ammonite on the ledges.

The track heads inland along the floor of Winspit Bottom. After 1km the valley divides. As you reach a pumping station bear right onto a wide path, which soon slants diagonally left up a long field to the edge of **Worth Matravers**. Through a gate, a fenced-in path runs up to become a lane of small houses.

The lane arrives at the village centre below a small garden. ◄ Cross this up to the street above, and head up to the right to the junction below the Square and Compass pub. Fork left, to the car park.

You could also follow the coast path another 1km to Seacombe and turn inland there.

The village is of Purbeck Limestone, with slightly different sorts used for paving, walls, lintels and roofing slabs.

WALK 29

Swanage: Durlston to Dancing Ledge

Start/Finish	Durleston Country Park SZ 032 773
Distance	16km (10 miles)
Ascent	300m (1000ft)
Approx time	4½hrs
Terrain	good paths, Swanage streets
Maps	Explorer OL15 Purbeck; Landranger 195 Bournemouth
Parking	large pay and display at Durleston

From Swanage, the old Priest's Way gets you quickly to Worth Matravers (but don't be too quick, as the Square and Compass only opens at midday). After a quick look around the village and the pub's fossil museum, the rest is coast walking on grassy paths above the low, chunky Portland Stone cliffs.

At Dancing Ledge are ammonites the size of dustbin lids – although the waves and people's feet have worn them down fairly shapeless. You could spot another at the approach to Durleston Head. And if you missed them in the wild, there are two good ones in the geological walkway, a few steps below the car park.

Start down the path towards Durlstone Castle, but immediately below the car park, at the top of the geological timescale descent, turn left in a wide, tree-shaded earth path. It runs gently downhill, with a wall on its right at the tops of cliffs. After 700 metres it bends inland (the disused path ahead has warning notices) and reaches the access road for Durleston Castle.

Turn right, in 300 metres turning right again following coast path signs in Bellevue Road. The 'Zigzag Path' descends to the right here to the fossil-rich foreshore. As the road bends left, turn right through a gateway to grassland. Descend along the line of yellow warnings alongside the cliffs. At the meadow foot, the Coast Path turns sharp left, but keep ahead to a signpost beside the watch tower on **Peveril Point**. ▶

PURBECK
PORTLAND

Below the signpost marked SZ040785 are the Purbeck Marble rocks with fossil snails.

PURBECK MARBLE

True marble is limestone after having been meta-morphosed – compressed, heated and hardened, usually by a mountain-building episode. It's uncommon in England, but found around the Mediterranean, where the Alpine Crunch has been building mountains and still is.

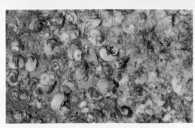

Purbeck Marble, with fossil snails, Peveril Point

Purbeck 'Marble' is normal, unmetamorphosed limestone, crammed with the fossils of freshwater snails (gastropods). It's called marble because it can be polished smooth, and this makes an ornamental stone especially loved by the builders of the Early English cathedrals of the 13th century. Salisbury Cathedral is rich in this snaily stone. It is seen in its natural state in the low cliff directly below the signpost marked 'SZ040785', and forms a reef out into the sea. At half tide, coming in or going out, a lively tiderace forms over this reef, and it's a hopeful spot for dolphin viewing.

Old pavements in Swanage also feature the Purbeck Marble: look for the greyish-coloured slabs.

Turn inland along a lane (there's also a foreshore option), past toilets. Just after a fancy block of flats on your right a path turns down right with steps to the sea-front. Turn left along the wide tarmac path, passing above the pier entrance (back right) and below a pair of Greek columns to the end of **Swanage** seafront.

Follow the tram lines along the esplanade. At the Museum and Heritage Centre there's an open area with fish and

chip shops. Bear left, inland, to the Square. Cross it into High Street.

At Earthlights Café keep left, signed for the Town Hall, into the pedestrianised section of High Street. At the end of the pedestrian zone keep ahead, passing the old market cross on your right and the Black Swan pub on your left. ▶

Ahead is an ancient cottage with stone-slab roof named 205 Parker's. Fork to left of the cottage, in Priest's Road. ▶ It becomes a residential street of semi-detached houses, running level and due west for 800 metres to a five-way junction.

Turn left, directly uphill, in Quarry Close. Slant up left across a parking area into a zone of static caravans. Bear right above Reception, up a tarmac track between caravans, then with caravans on your left and a hedge on your right. At the top of the hedge and before caravans recommence on the right, take a gap on the right.

A grass track leads along the foot of a campsite to another lane – a drinking water tap is on the left here. Turn up the lane for 15 metres, then right on a path through a wood. The path continues fenced on both sides, to turn downhill briefly to a track corner. Here turn back up left, to pass through a gate above Belle Vue Farm.

The hedged, rough track contours across the downland flank, with views across Swanage

Greyer-coloured pavement slabs are Purbeck Marble, with the fossil snails.

This is the ancient Priest's Way arriving in the town.

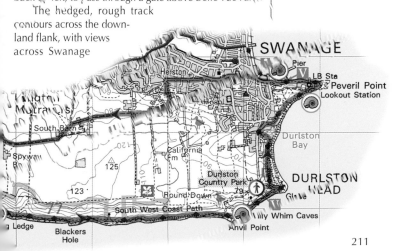

to the sea and Ballard Down. It becomes tarmac for 200 metres, to a junction where it turns down right and a rougher track turns up left; here take the stile directly ahead.

A path slants slightly left across a field to another track junction. Take the track ahead (west), with a large hay barn on your right. This is the **Priest's Way**, and you'll be following it for the next 3km towards Worth Matravers.

After 800 metres the track bends left to a nearby house (**Spyway Barn**) but keep ahead on the smaller track. You pass a side track for Dancing Ledge on your left, then a quarry area on your right. Finally you pass **Eastington Farm** on your left to a gate where the track, which has been walled in on both sides, emerges into an open field.

Bear left off the track, with a wall and then a fence on your left, to a small gate. The path continues across small fields through gates, to reach the road at the northeastern edge of **Worth Matravers**. Head down left into the village. Follow the road down to the crossroads at the Square and Compass pub.

Portland Stone cliffs, Seacombe Cliff

Mud cracks in Purbeck Stone, in the garden of the Square and Compass pub, Worth Matravers

The **Square and Compass** serves real ales and cider, and very good home-made pasties (but not full meals). The outside tables are awkward for balancing beer mugs, as they're slabs of Purbeck Limestone with polygonal raised ridges. These are sun-dried mud, the cracks refilled with gritty sediment, and then preserved as rock for 150 million years. The pub garden also has large ammonites and a dinosaur footprint.

Inside, the pub has a remarkable fossil collection, the result of 60 years of collecting by two generations of publicans. There are fine ammonites, as well as sea-dinosaurs (ichthyosaur and pliosaur), all displayed in the jumbled-together style of an old-fashioned museum. This can be enjoyed free, and with a glass of beer in your hand. Summer opening noon until 11.00pm daily.

In another 50 metres, another lane, London Row, is signed for the coast path at Winspit. This adds 1km of extra (coast) walking and the ammonites of Winspit Quarry.

Follow the road downhill for 100 metres, to a lane back to the left signposted for 'Seacombe'. ◄ In a few steps a path turns off to the left, emerging into a wide grassy valley.

Head straight across the valley hollow, east, to a stile on the skyline. The path descends into the next valley hollow. After a gate it slants down to the right, with steps, through bramble and elder. A wide path continues down the floor of the valley.

At a stone marker, take the main path, forking left. Soon the Coast Path joins out of the low trees to right of the path. Keep the fence on your right, ignoring a field gate in it, to reach the top of **Seacombe Cliff**.

Turn left along the cliff top path. After 600 metres, the path forks left through a kissing gate. It passes around the head of a quarried hollow that looks as if it might be Dancing Ledge but isn't. In another 500 metres, a stile on the right lets you down onto **Dancing Ledge**, a semi-circle of quarry floor overlooking the sea. If the tide is low enough, you can scramble down from the quarry rim onto a lower ledge, with a swimming pool hollow and sea-washed giant ammonites.

A fairly poor ammonite is in the gate post.

Return to the stile above Dancing Ledge and continue to the right along the cliff top path. It rises slightly through scrub and gorse, then drops back to the top of the chunky Portland Stone cliff. Soon you pass the lower of the double indicator posts at the west end of the measured mile for shipping. In another 500 metres the path passes below a wall end. ◄

After 1km you arrive at Anvil Point, keeping just below the wall around the lighthouse and dropping to cross a dry valley, with the quarry holes of Tilly Whim Caves seen ahead.

A ledge with a **blowhole** crack is a short scramble down to the right: in stormy weather waves squirt up through this. At the point where you step down onto the platform is a foot-worn ammonite 30cm wide.

DANCING LEDGE

Dancing Ledge is a former quarry in the Portland Stone, now a sheltered picnic spot also popular with rock climbers.

The lower ledge is exposed as the tide goes down, and can be reached by a short down-scramble. This ledge is the top surface of the so-called Prickle Bed: the 'prickly' texture is fossil crab burrows. Elsewhere, the Prickle Bed top is the 'Puffin Ledge', perched on by birds rather than people. Here it has a swimming pool carved out of it, and several sea-washed ammonites about 50cm wide. Having scrambled down, if you look underneath the ledges along the platform back, a few steps to the west of the scrambling-down place, you may find a corner of a better preserved one.

The rock wall between the two levels shows exuberant chert: glassy blackish lumps within the pale yellowish stones. Chert is chemically similar to the flints in chalk, and is probably formed in the same way: silica from marine sponges, originally their skeletal spines, self-assembling by migrating through the sediments as they formed into rock.

East of the ledges, beyond a sea cave, lime-rich underground water has been seeping out and then evaporating, to form flowstone or tufa: a limestone layer smeared onto the rock. Varying amounts of iron in the underground water give the flowstone a range of beige to orange and black colours.

Across the dry stream bed, the path heads up above the cave holes. The wide main path runs level, between walls guarding the upper entrances to **Tilly Whim Caves**. It passes a viewpoint with birdlife indicator boards,

Blowhole, Tilly Whim

then passes below a stone globe, to a sharp bend above **Durleston Head**. Now it climbs (ignoring an old path off right, lost in cliff collapse) to the entrance to Durleston Castle. Keep uphill on a winding path with geological timescale. At the top this passes between tall lumps of Portland Stone with large ammonites and oyster-type shells. The car park is just above.

WALK 30
Ballard Down and Agglestone

Start/Finish	Ulwell, at the north edge of Swanage SZ 021 809
Distance	11.5km (7 miles)
Ascent	250m (800ft)
Approx time	3½hrs
Terrain	good path and lanes, sandy foreshore, sandy small paths on Studland Heath
Maps	Explorer OL15 Purbeck; Landranger 195 Bournemouth
Parking	at the north end of Ulwell: the southern of the two pull-offs

The Jurassic Coast officially ends at the spectacular sea stack of Old Harry. But the coastal path continues into the last of the geological periods, the Tertiary, here displaying itself as a striking red-and-yellow sandstone formed by great rivers that once flowed on top of the chalk.

Along with the sandstone lump called Agglestone and the chalk stacks of Old Harry, the walk covers downland and heathland, and a popular sandy beach.

From the back of the parking area a kissing gate leads to a path slanting left up through woods. At a path junction, keep ahead up a steep path with steps to the **obelisk** at the crest of **Ballard Down**. Turn right, on the wide path along the crest of the down. After a short rise, you head gently down, with the Isle of Wight ahead. After a gate, you reach the trig point. Bear right, through a nearby gate, and continue down the down end with a fence on your left.

The wide path runs along grassy cliff tops, with vertical chalk and sea stacks on the right, to a trampled corner alongside **Old Harry Rocks**. Turn sharp left (there's nowhere else to turn) along the north-facing shoreline. The wide, well-used path runs into scrub, then along an open field. Keep ahead as the path becomes a roughly

Agglestone Grit

CHALK

Old Harry Rocks

Access down right to the beach and Redend Point is currently closed.

tarred driveway, then meets a small road at the edge of **Studland**.

Turn right, past the Bankes Arms on your left. Opposite a National Trust car park, turn right onto a small path. At the low cliff top this bends left. ◀ The path follows a field edge then is under trees, passing above **Redend Point**. It bends inland beside a large concrete observation bunker.

> **Fort Henry**, a Grade II listed building protected by the NT, is where Churchill, King George, Monty (Field Marshal Bernard Montgomery of Alamein) and Admiral Mountbatten watched live-ammunition rehearsals for D Day on the beach below.
>
> Down on the beach, Redend Point has the same red and orange river sandstone as the Agglestone.

When the path emerges alongside a car park, turn sharp right down to the beach. Turn left along the beach. If the tide's in, leaving only soft dry sand to walk in, there's a path just inland among the beach huts. After 800 metres, just after a row of brown beach huts, you reach the busy

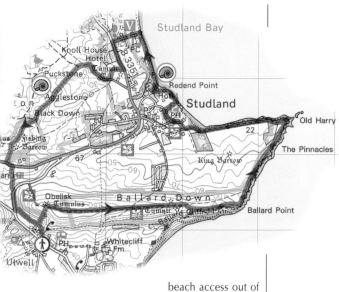

beach access out of
the main NT car park, with café
and other buildings. Head inland on the car park access
track to **B3351** road, and turn left along the verge. Some
200 metres after **Knoll House Hotel**, cross to a black gate
with bridleway signpost. The hedged, wide path runs for
150 metres. At its end, bear left to a hedge gap and a
stony track beyond.

Turn right, descending into woods to cross a footbridge. At once turn left on a wide, sandy path. After
100 metres and just before leaving the trees, fork left
on a small path with yellow waymark arrow. It emerges
onto open heathland, heading to the strange upstanding
Agglestone ahead.

The bedding in the **Agglestone**'s red-and-yellow
sandstone shows two things. First, the tor has fallen
over (this happened about 50 years ago). Second,
the cross-bedded (tilted) strata within the general
layering indicate sandbars in a lively river.

Agglestone on Studland Heath: riverbed gravel from the Tertiary, the most recent of the geological periods

From the tor the path continues southwest to a track junction. Bear slightly right ('Studland Road') through a gate. The path leads between tall gorse bushes out across a golf course, but the gorse is so tall that you see no golfers, just the occasional small ball flying overhead. Bear right as the path joins a wider one running through the golf course. It bends slightly left, to reach the road beyond.

Turn left for 50 metres to a stile on the other side. A faint path leads out across more of the golf course: aim for the middle of a small wood beyond the fairway. A stile leads to a path down through it. At the wood foot, keep straight downhill to a stile leading onto the road at the base of **Ballard Down**.

Turn right for 300 metres to a junction. On the left, a short track leads to a path (signed 'Old Harry') on the right. It contours through woods to the path junction at the start of the walk. Turn down right, to the Ulwell parking area.

THE ISLE OF PURBECK CIRCUIT

The 'Alpine Crunch' that lifted the rocks of Durdle Door through 90° also affected the chalk country inland. From Ballard Point to Corfe Castle, the bedrock has been faulted and lifted in a structure resembling a breaking wave. This forms the high ridgeline that separates the so-called 'Isle' of Portland from the rest of Dorset. The Purbeck ridge offers a life-enhancing all-day walk that includes the charms of Corfe Castle; the pub at Worth Matravers famed alike for its fossils and its home-made pasties; giant ammonites at Dancing Ledge; and Purbeck's own stone, the snail-filled Purbeck Marble, at Peveril Point. The magnificent rampage is 27.5km (17 miles) long with 650m (2100ft) of ascent – taking about 8 hours.

Start at Ulwell, at the northern edge of **Swanage** (SZ 020 810, easier to get to than Durlestone). Follow the ridgeline west to **Corfe Castle**. Head south over the Wealden Clay valley, with a harder sandstone band forming Corfe Common.

Cross the B3069 road 1km east of Kingston, for a path that drops into **Coombe Bottom**, with a side-bottom leading up to **Worth Matravers**. Follow Walk 29 by Dancing Ledge, to its end at Durleston Castle. Then start again at its beginning, by **Peveril Point** to Swanage sea-front. The Coast Path revisits the Wealdon Clay below New Swanage and heads up onto **Ballard Down**. Turn west along the chalk ridgeline back to Ulwell.

Corfe Castle from Challow Hill

APPENDIX A

Route summary table

No	Start/Finish	Distance	Ascent	Time	Page
1	East Budleigh	19km (11 miles)	300m (1000ft)	5¼hrs	31
2	East Budleigh	12.5km (7½ miles)	200m (650ft)	3½hrs	37
3	Otterton	21km (13 miles); or 12km (7½ miles)	400m (1400ft); or 250m (800ft)	6hrs; or 3½hrs	42
4	Sidmouth	14km (9 miles); or 12km (7½ miles)	450m (1500ft); or 200m (700ft)	4½hrs; or 3hrs	49
5	Branscombe Mouth	12km (7½ miles)	350m (1200ft)	4hrs	56
6	Beer (or Branscombe Mouth)	6.5km (4 miles)	300m (1000ft)	2½hrs	61
7	Luppitt/Dumpdon Hill	7.5km (4½ miles)/1.5km (1 mile)	250m (800ft)/50m (150ft)	2¼hrs/45mins	65
8	Axmouth Bridge/ Lyme Regis	10.5km (6½ miles)	300m (1000ft)	4hrs	74
9	Lyme Regis	9.5km (6 miles)	250m (800ft)	3hrs	80
10	West of Chideock	12km (7½ miles); or 10km (6 miles)	550m (1800ft); or 400m (1300ft)	4hrs; or 3¼hrs	87
11	West of Chideock	5km (3 miles)	200m (650ft)	2hrs	92
12	West Bay	15km (9 miles); or 13km (8 miles)	450m (1500ft); or 400m (1400ft)	4½hrs; or 4hrs	96
13	West Bay	14km (8½ miles)	250m (800ft)	4hrs	105
14	Beaminster	19km (12 miles); or 21km (13 miles)	500m (1650ft)	6hrs; or 6½hrs	112
15	Eggardon Hill	14.5km (9 miles)	500m (1650ft)	4½hrs	121

No	Start/Finish	Distance	Ascent	Time	Page
16	Abbotsbury	18km (11 miles); or 13km (8 miles)	300m (1000ft); or 250m (800ft)	5hrs; or 4¼hrs	127
17	Hardy Monument, near Dorchester	14.5km (9 miles)	300m (1000ft)	4½hrs	134
18	Isle of Portland	13.5km (8½ miles)	150m (500ft)	4hrs	139
19	Preston	14.5km (9 miles); or 13km (8 miles)	350m (1200ft)	4½hrs; or 4hrs	145
20	Minterne Magna	21.5km (13½ miles); or 14.5km (9 miles)	300m (900ft); or 250m (800ft)	6hrs; or 4hrs	153
21	Woolland Hill	25.5km (16 miles)	550m (1800ft)	7½hrs	161
22	Shillingstone	17km (10½ miles)	400m (1400ft)	5hrs	171
23	Ringstead	11.5km (7 miles); 5.5km (3.5 miles)	250m (800ft); or 150m (500ft)	3½hrs; or 2hrs	176
24	Lulworth	10.5km (6½ miles)	400m (1400ft)	3½hrs	182
25	Lulworth	6km (3¾ miles)	250m (800ft)	2hrs	187
26	Kimmeridge	14km (9 miles); or 11.5km (7 miles); or 8.5km (5 miles)	450m (1500ft); or 300m (1000ft); or 150m (500ft)	4½hrs; or 3½hrs; or 2½hrs	193
27	Kimmeridge	14km (8½ miles); or 8km (5 miles)	350m (1100ft); or 250m (800ft)	4½hrs; or 2½hrs	199
28	Worth Matravers	9.5km (6 miles); or 6km (3½miles)	300m (1000ft); or 150m (500ft)	3hrs; or 2hrs	204
29	Durleston Country Park, Swanage	16km (10 miles)	300m (1000ft)	4½hrs	209
30	Ulwell, Swanage	11.5km (7 miles)	250m (800ft)	3½hrs	217

APPENDIX B

Indoor Geology: Museums and visitor centres

As well as the ammonites and shells you find for yourself on the beach, it's good to see the rarer and better preserved ones in the area's museums; especially if it's a nasty wet day.

Bridport

Small town museum in fine 16th-century building. Local fossils including a brittle star from the Starfish Bed, Bridport rope and net industry, local history. Limited opening Oct–March, closed Sundays and all January, free. www.bridportmuseum.co.uk.

Budleigh Salterton

The thatched Fairlynch Museum. Selection of Budleigh Salterton pebbles and an Ordovician fossil found inside one of them. Open 2.00pm–4.30pm, closed Mondays and in winter. www.fairlynchmuseum.uk.

Charmouth

Charmouth Heritage Coast Centre. Displays of commonplace fossils rather than museum specimens. Well informed and helpful staff will identify your finds. Fossil walks most days in summer, times depend on tides. A very good centre, up on 1st floor (commercial fossil shop downstairs). Open summer daily 10.30am–4.30pm, winter Friday–Monday 10.30am–4.30pm. www.charmouth.org/chcc.

Dorchester

Dorset County Museum. Small but well-chosen fossil display, including a cast of Mary Anning's plesiosaur's head. Reconstructed Thomas Hardy study, and local history. Open Monday–Saturday summer 10am–5pm, winter 10am–4pm (NB closed for redevelopment until Summer 2020). www.dorsetcountymuseum.org.

Exeter

Royal Albert Museum. Best place for the rare fossils (including Woody the Rhynchosaur) of the Triassic Red Beds; also Torbay limestone corals. Tuesday–Sunday 10am–5pm. www.rammuseum.org.uk.

Kimmeridge

The Etches Collection. Opened in 2017, specially built to house the outstanding collection of 2000 fossils from the Kimmeridge Clay collected and conserved by local plumber Steve Etches. www.theetchescollection.org.

Lulworth

Lulworth Cove Visitor Centre. Good displays and maps explaining local geology, and a small collection of Kimmeridge fossils. Open 10.00am daily, closed Christmas Day.

Lyme Regis

Dinosaurland Fossil Museum in Coombe Street (okay, it really ought to be 'Ichthyosaurland') a couple of blocks in from the sea, which prides itself on showing lots of fossils, mostly collected locally by museum owner Steve Davies. Over 12,000 exhibits, including several ichythosaurs. Open 10am–4pm summer daily, winter Saturday–Sunday. www.dinosaurland.co.uk.

Lyme Regis Museum. Local history and literature as well as geology. Guided fossil walks 15–20 days a month depending on tides. Open summer Monday–Saturday 10am–5pm, Sunday 11am–4pm, winter Wednesday–Sunday 11am–4pm. www.lymeregismuseum.co.uk.

Portland

Portland Museum. Small, thatched building with big ammonites, good on cycads (Jurassic trees). Open daily 10.30am–4pm, closed winter.

www.portlandmuseum.co.uk.

Sidmouth

Sidmouth Museum. Local history, Sir Arthur Conan Doyle, and a room of geology including rhynchosaur bits. (Red Bed fossils are rare, even inside the museum...) Closed Sundays, Monday mornings, and during the winter.

Swanage

Museum and Heritage Centre. Small, volunteer-run museum on the seafront. Fossils (especially dinosaur footprints) collected by a local schoolteacher. Open daily 10am–5pm, 10.30–4.30, shorter hours or closed winter. swanagemuseum.uk.

Worth Matravers

One room at the Square & Compass pub is jammed with the local fossil collections of two generations of pub landlords. Unlike other museums, this one opens until 11pm and you're allowed to bring in beer. Bigger items such as dinosaur footprints are out in the garden. www.squareandcompasspub.co.uk.

APPENDIX C

Rock reference

In print

Exploring the Undercliffs
by Donald Campbell.
Coastal Publishing (2000)
Inexpensive nicely produced booklet supplementing the Official Guide (see below) with more detail on the Lyme Regis Undercliff.

Geology of South Dorset and southeast Devon and its World Heritage Coast
MA Woods, et al. British Geological Survey Memoir (2011)
Definitive but very technical.

The Isle of Purbeck
by Paul Ensom and Malcolm Turnbull.
Coastal Publishing (2011)
Another of the detail guides supplementing the Official Guide. Out of print so snap it up second-hand.

The Official Guide to the Jurassic Coast
editor Prof Denys Brunsden.
Coastal Publishing (2003)
A useful short summary with attractive pictures; the outstanding 3m-wide cliff diagram can be carried in a map case on all walks. Out of print (and getting pricy second-hand)

Sandstone & Sea Stacks
by Ronald Turnbull. Frances Lincoln (2011)
Large-format picture book covering the UK coast as a whole.

Online

animation: 'The Jurassic Coast a Mighty Tale' to fill 5 mins by Tim Brotton
Catch YouTube or the Jurassic Coast website.

app: iGeology
from British Geological Survey
Free download for Android/iOS/Kindle operating system, all UK bedrock superimposed on OS Landranger mapping, for current location or search by place name or grid reference.

pdf download: *Dorset Building Stones Atlas* by Jo Pennell (English Heritage)
Free download – search by its name

website: *Geology of the Wessex Coast* at www.southampton.ac.uk by Dr Ian West 150 web pages, 10,000 images, 20 years of research. An immensely detailed survey of the whole coast, at undergraduate geologist level.

website: The official Jurassic Coast website at www.jurassiccoast.org
General info for coast visitors, a survey of the area's museums, and an illustrated database of 1000 local fossils.

website: *Geology of Britain Viewer* at www.bgs.ac.uk
Bedrock for all Britain, at 1:50,000 scale. Click 'bedrock only' for clarity.

website: Lexicon of named rock units www.bgs.ac.uk
Further details of the rock layers as found on the iGeology website or app.

website: English Riviera Geopark www.englishrivierageopark.org.uk
The Devonian (and other) rocks of Torbay, to west of the walks in this book, and a rich area for a whole new geological period. General visitor information and a good introduction to the rocks.

APPENDIX D

Glossary of geological terms

Term	Definition
aragonite	the 'mother-of-pearl' mineral forming some shell fossils including ammonites and gastropods (whelks). Chemically the same as calcite, but softer, and more liable to dissolve in sea water (see Walk 20).
belemnite	squid-like creature living in the Jurassic sea. Its internal shell skeleton forms a fossil like an elongated bullet (see Walk 11).
bioturbation	term for rock churned up by burrowing creatures, useful when we're not sure whether the creatures were worms, shrimps or whatever.
bivalve	see brachiopod.
brachiopod	evolution has invented seashells twice: bivalves, and brachiopods. Brachiopods (lamp shells) have upper and lower shells which are dissimilar, although each is symmetrical left-to-right. Bivalves have left and right shells each a reflection of the other. Both bivalves and brachiopods were common in the Jurassic; today's beach seashells are all bivalves (apart from whelks, which are gastropods).
calcite	a white mineral (calcium carbonate), usually lumpy but sometimes crystalline, which forms limestone, limescale in kettles, and many shelly fossils.
chert	hard, slightly translucent, greyish or yellowish lumps of silica that assemble themselves (as concretions) during the process of rock formation. Found in the Upper Greenstone, and the Portland Limestone. Flint is a particular form of chert (Walk 15).
clay	older geologists use 'clay' also for rock formed from clay, what's today usually called mudstone.

Term	Definition
concretion	during the heating and compression of rock formation, minerals can be liberated to form chunks within the rock. Flints and cherts are concretions of silica; other concretions are of red iron oxide or limestone calcite (Walk 19).
cross-bedding	sandstone beds laid down on the slant, having formed in river or sea bed sandbanks, or desert dunes.
dolomite	like limestone, but with magnesium replacing calcium. Nothing to do with dolerite, which is a dark, basalt-family volcanic rock (Walk 27).
gastropods	curly, spiral seashells of the snail or whelk family.
glauconite	the iron mineral that gives a greenish colour to freshly quarried Greensand sandstone. It forms on a stagnant, oxygen-starved sea bed. Exposed to the air, it weathers ('rusts'), so that Greensand is usually yellowish brown (Walks 4, 14).
Ham Stone	golden limestone, part of the Inferior Oolite, widely used in Dorset buildings (Walk 21).
marble	geologically, a tough, hard rock formed by compression and heating of limestone in mountain-building events. The Jurassic Coast has no true marble. More loosely 'marble' is any hardish limestone that looks nice when cut and polished (Forest Marble, Walk 17; Purbeck Marble, Walk 29).
marl	clay soil with high lime content or rock formed from such a mix. Intermediate between limestone and mudstone.
rhizoconcretion	shapes of former tree roots preserved in calcite mineral, found in red desert sandstone around Budleigh Salterton (Walk 7).
oolite	rock formed from tiny, rounded grains of pure limestone, such as form white beaches of the Bahamas today (Walk 16).
silcrete	flints cemented with silica mineral into boulder-size lumps ('sarsen stones') sometimes used for stone circles. The flints are from the chalk, but the silica lumps formed in hot, wet-and-dry climate during the more recent Tertiary period.
silica	a hard white mineral (silicon dioxide) that makes up lumps of chert (in some sandstones and limestones) and flint (in chalk). Its crystalline form is quartz.
stromatolite	lumps of algal slime stiffened with layers of calcite – this limestone 'skeleton' is preserved as fossils. Possibly Earth's most important lifeform: through 2 billion years of the Precambrian the algae created earth's oxygen. It's found today in a few brackish pools in Australia (Walk 25).
trace fossil	a fossil that's just a mark left by a living creature, for example worm holes, dinosaur footprints
unconformity	a junction between two rock beds that represents a gap in time. The surface of the lower rock has been worn down and eroded before the arrival of the much younger rock on top (see Introduction).

APPENDIX E

Timechart: Cambrian period to the present day

A quick timechart of all eleven geological periods, for when we can't quite remember what did come after the Carboniferous, together with the main earth-shaking events affecting Dorset. Timescale is millions of years.

Period	Events	Scale
Tertiary	Ice Age *Alpine Crunch* Atlantic Ocean opens extinction of dinosaurs, ammonites	**now**
Cretaceous	The Chalk The Greensand Chalk sea cuts across S England	**–100**
Jurassic	Portland Stone The Lias	**–200**
Triassic	first dinosaurs, ammonites **The New Red Sandstone**	
Permian	Pangaea world continent *Variscan Crunch*	
Carboniferous	Coal Measures UK crossing equator Mountain Limestone	**–300**
Devonian	The Old Red Sandstone	
Silurian	*Caledonian Crunch* *Scotland :: England*	**–400**
Ordovician		
		–500
Cambrian	first life with shells	
Precambrian	another 3000 million years	**–600**

Rocks of the Jurassic Coast

The rocks are grouped here in 'geological' order (Tertiary, Cretaceous, Jurassic and Triassic), with the youngest at the top. This means that the red beds of Devon, in the east and in the early part of the book, appear at the end of this list.

The British Geological Survey's iGeology app lists 68 rock formations along the Jurassic Coast (and even those can be analysed down to individual beds, like the Portland Roach or the Cinder Bed at Lulworth). I've used broader classifications and focused on the more easily recognisable sorts of stone. At Sidford, the BGS app has 'Sidmouth Mudstone'; if you click through to the Lexicon of Named Rock Units, you'll see the Mercia Mudstone, as mentioned here, is the parent unit. To complicate things further, many older geologists and heritage websites use the Mercia Mudstone's older name, Keuper Marl.

Tertiary

Agglestone Grit — Soft, red and orange riverbed sandstone, with ironstone concretions. Elsewhere in Dorset Tertiary rocks include Poole Formation, London Clay, etc: riverbed sand, gravel and clay.

Cretaceous

CHALK — Pure white limestone formed of microscopic fossils (coccoliths). Visible fossils (sea urchins) aren't easily found. Flints (silica concretions).

GREENSAND — **Upper Greensand:** pale brown shelly sandstone, sometimes with green mineral glauconite indicating a stagnant, oxygen-starved sea bed. Chert concretions common.

Gault: dark clay with ammonites. In cliffs the narrow Gault layer is usually overgrown with scrubby trees.

WEALDEN clay — Clay from shallow lake beds, in cheerful colours of red/orange/purple suggesting they've been washed from land that's hot with only occasional rain. Often with scraps of fossil timber (lignite).

Jurassic (upper)

PURBECK

Limestone from saltwater lagoons. At its top the distinctive **Purbeck Marble** with freshwater snails (Gastropods). Lower down are **Broken Beds**, above the Fossil Forest tree casts with fossil soil levels.

PORTLAND

Portland Stone: pale oolitic limestone, firm and resisting erosion. Oolite is limestone beach sand, formed in warm climates. The top layer is **Roach**, with shelly fossils including the spiral Portland Screw (Turitella gastropod). The building stone is **Portland Freestone**, smooth and featureless. Giant ammonites, chert, scallop shells.

Portland Sands: softer clay and sandstone.

Kimmeridge Clay

Dark-cloured mudstone, from an anaerobic (oxygen-starved) sea bed, with oil shale, limestone and dolomite bands. Ammonites.

CORALLIAN

Shallow coastal water mix-up of limestone, mudstone, sandstone and clay. Shells, large ovoid Dogger concretions, worm and shrimp burrows and some coral.

Jurassic (mid and lower)

OXFORD Clay

Grey clay and mudstone, with ammonites.

middle Jurassic

Mostly clay with some harder bands. In shallower water, from Somerset northwards, the corresponding layer is the Great Oolite.

Cornbrash: yellow, rubbly, hard sandstone/limestone interbedded with cream-coloured mudstone.

Forest Marble

Forest Marble: hard, pale grey, shelly limestone rich in oysters, formed from shell banks in a shallow sea.

Frome Clay: dark grey, very sticky clay, formerly 'upper Fuller's Earth'.

Inferior Oolite

Yellow or orange oolitic limestone crammed with ammonites, belemnites and shells, with reddish 'snuffbox' concretions.

Jurassic (mid and lower) - continued

Bridport Sands

Layered yellow sandstone, with fossil wormholes in the harder layers.

upper Lias

Clay and drab sandstone. **Down Cliff Clay;** the narrow **Junction Bed** (now called 'Beacon Limestone Formation') hard limestone with shells; yellow **Thorncombe Sand** with Dogger concretions; **Down Cliff Sand**; grey **Eype Clay**.

Charmouth Mdstn

Grey shale, mudstone and clay, rich in ammonites, belemnites and shells, with occasional plesiosaurs. Includes **Green Ammonite Beds**, **Belemnite Marls**, **Black Ven Marls**, **Shales with Beef**.

BLUE LIAS

Layered grey mudstone/limestone, with many fossils including large ammonites.

Triassic

PENARTH Group

Mudstone, limestone, sandstone, mostly hidden under Lyme Regis Undercliff landslips. **White Lias** at the top; **Tea Green Marls** at the foot.

MERCIA Mudstn

Old name 'Keuper Marls'. Soft red mudstone from seasonal desert lakes, with white or pink gypsum streaks and grey-green reduction bands.

OTTER Sandstone

Red desert sandstone from dunes and, more layered, from flash floods. Carbonate plant-root shapes (rhizoconcretions)

B S Pebble Beds

Cobblestones (mostly hard, off-white quartzite) from a very large river bed, loosely bound in a red sandstone.

Aylesbeare Mdstn

Red desert sandstone from dunes and flash floods, and lake-bed mudstone.

APPENDIX G

Jurassic Coast cliff diagrams

JURASSIC COAST WEST: Exmouth to Chesil Beach

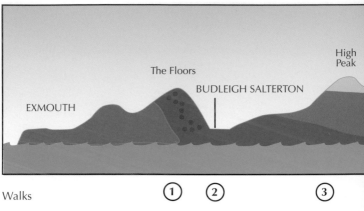

Walks ① ② ③

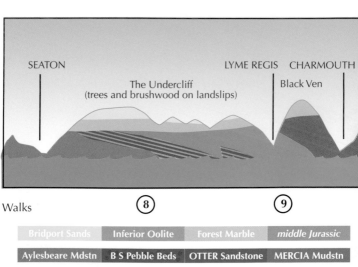

Walks ⑧ ⑨

Bridport Sands	Inferior Oolite	Forest Marble	*middle Jurassic*
Aylesbeare Mdstn	B S Pebble Beds	OTTER Sandstone	MERCIA Mudstn

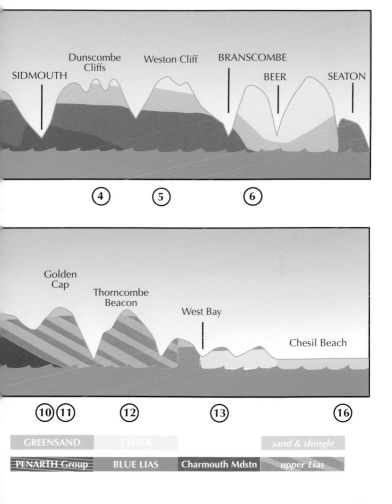

233

JURASSIC COAST EAST: Chesil Beach to Studland

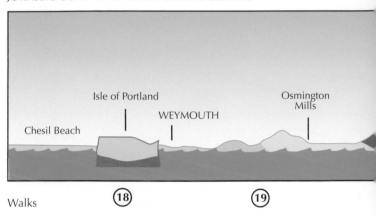

Walks ⑱ ⑲

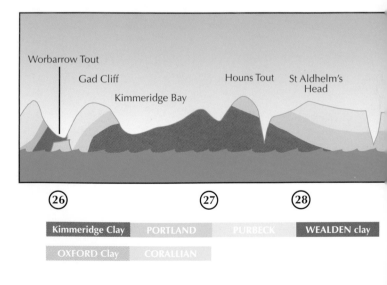

⑲ ⑳

| Kimmeridge Clay | PORTLAND | PURBECK | WEALDEN clay |

| OXFORD Clay | CORALLIAN |

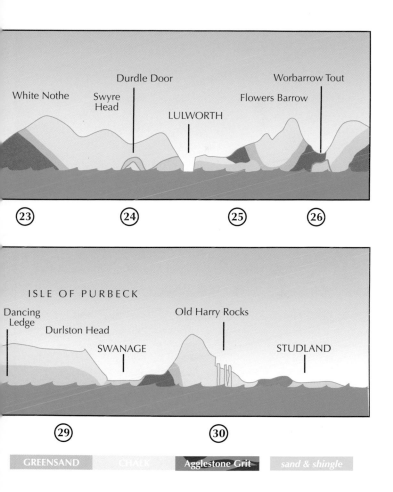

Path from Seatown to Golden Cap, the highest point of the south coast

DOWNLOAD THE ROUTES
IN GPX FORMAT

All the routes in this guide are available for download from:

www.cicerone.co.uk/741/GPX

as GPX files. You should be able to load them into most formats of mobile device, whether GPS or smartphone.

When you go to this link, you will be asked for your email address and where you purchased the guide, and have the option to subscribe to the Cicerone e-newsletter.

Note that recent small diversions on Routes 8 and 25 are not incorporated into the GPX files – follow Coast Path markers.

www.cicerone.co.uk

LISTING OF CICERONE GUIDES

DERBYSHIRE, PEAK DISTRICT AND MIDLANDS

Cycling in the Peak District
Dark Peak Walks
Scrambles in the Dark Peak
Walking in Derbyshire
White Peak Walks:
    The Northern Dales
White Peak Walks:
    The Southern Dales

SOUTHERN ENGLAND

20 Classic Sportive Rides in South East England
20 Classic Sportive Rides in South West England
Cycling in the Cotswolds
Mountain Biking on the North Downs
Mountain Biking on the South Downs
North Downs Way Map Booklet
South West Coast Path Map Booklet – Vol 1: Minehead to St Ives
South West Coast Path Map Booklet – Vol 2: St Ives to Plymouth
South West Coast Path Map Booklet – Vol 3: Plymouth to Poole
Suffolk Coast and Heath Walks
The Cotswold Way
The Cotswold Way Map Booklet
The Great Stones Way
The Kennet and Avon Canal
The Lea Valley Walk
The North Downs Way
The Peddars Way and Norfolk Coast path
The Pilgrims' Way
The Ridgeway Map Booklet
The Ridgeway National Trail
The South Downs Way
The South Downs Way Map Booklet
The South West Coast Path
The Thames Path
The Thames Path Map Booklet
The Two Moors Way
Two Moors Way Map Booklet
Walking Hampshire's Test Way
Walking in Cornwall
Walking in Essex
Walking in Kent
Walking in London
Walking in Norfolk
Walking in Sussex
Walking in the Chilterns
Walking in the Cotswolds
Walking in the Isles of Scilly
Walking in the New Forest

Walking in the North Wessex Downs
Walking in the Thames Valley
Walking on Dartmoor
Walking on Guernsey
Walking on Jersey
Walking on the Isle of Wight
Walking the Jurassic Coast
Walks in the South Downs National Park

BRITISH ISLES CHALLENGES, COLLECTIONS AND ACTIVITIES

The Book of the Bivvy
The Book of the Bothy
The C2C Cycle Route
The End to End Cycle Route
The Mountains of England and Wales: Vol 1 Wales
The Mountains of England and Wales: Vol 2 England
The National Trails
The UK's County Tops
Three Peaks, Ten Tors

ALPS CROSS-BORDER ROUTES

100 Hut Walks in the Alps
Across the Eastern Alps: E5
Alpine Ski Mountaineering Vol 1 – Western Alps
Alpine Ski Mountaineering Vol 2 – Central and Eastern Alps
Chamonix to Zermatt
The Karnischer Hohenweg
The Tour of the Bernina
Tour of Mont Blanc
Tour of Monte Rosa
Tour of the Matterhorn
Trail Running – Chamonix and the Mont Blanc region
Trekking in the Alps
Trekking in the Silvretta and Rätikon Alps
Trekking Munich to Venice
Walking in the Alps

PYRENEES AND FRANCE/SPAIN CROSS-BORDER ROUTES

The GR10 Trail
The GR11 Trail
The Pyrenean Haute Route
The Pyrenees
The Way of St James – Spain
Walks and Climbs in the Pyrenees

AUSTRIA

Innsbruck Mountain Adventures
The Adlerweg
Trekking in Austria's Hohe Tauern
Trekking in the Stubai Alps
Trekking in the Zillertal Alps
Walking in Austria

SWITZERLAND

Cycle Touring in Switzerland
Switzerland's Jura Crest Trail
The Swiss Alpine Pass Route – Via Alpina Route 1
The Swiss Alps
Tour of the Jungfrau Region
Walking in the Bernese Oberland
Walking in the Valais

FRANCE AND BELGIUM

Chamonix Mountain Adventures
Cycle Touring in France
Cycling London to Paris
Cycling the Canal de la Garonne
Cycling the Canal du Midi
Écrins National Park
Mont Blanc Walks
Mountain Adventures in the Maurienne
The GR20 Corsica
The GR5 Trail
The GR5 Trail – Vosges and Jura
The Grand Traverse of the Massif Central
The Loire Cycle Route
The Moselle Cycle Route
The River Rhone Cycle Route
The Robert Louis Stevenson Trail
The Way of St James – Le Puy to the Pyrenees
Tour of the Oisans: The GR54
Tour of the Queyras
Vanoise Ski Touring
Via Ferratas of the French Alps
Walking in Corsica
Walking in Provence – East
Walking in Provence – West
Walking in the Auvergne
Walking in the Briançonnais
Walking in the Cevennes
Walking in the Dordogne
Walking in the Haute Savoie: North
Walking in the Haute Savoie: South
Walks in the Cathar Region
The GR5 Trail – Benelux and Lorraine
Walking in the Ardennes

GERMANY

Hiking and Cycling in the Black Forest
The Danube Cycleway Vol 1
The Rhine Cycle Route
The Westweg
Walking in the Bavarian Alps

ICELAND AND GREENLAND

Trekking in Greenland – The Arctic Circle Trail
Walking and Trekking in Iceland

For full information on all our
guides, books and eBooks,
visit our website:
www.cicerone.co.uk

Walking – Trekking – Mountaineering – Climbing – Cycling

Over 40 years, Cicerone have built up an outstanding collection of over 300 guides, inspiring all sorts of amazing adventures.

 Every guide comes from extensive exploration and research by our expert authors, all with a passion for their subjects. They are frequently praised, endorsed and used by clubs, instructors and outdoor organisations.

All our titles can now be bought as **e-books**, **ePubs** and **Kindle** files and we also have an online magazine – **Cicerone Extra** – with features to help cyclists, climbers, walkers and trekkers choose their next adventure, at home or abroad.

Our website shows any **new information** we've had in since a book was published. Please do let us know if you find anything has changed, so that we can publish the latest details. On our **website** you'll also find great ideas and lots of detailed information about what's inside every guide and you can buy **individual routes** from many of them online.

It's easy to keep in touch with what's going on at Cicerone by getting our monthly **free e-newsletter**, which is full of offers, competitions, up-to-date information and topical articles. You can subscribe on our home page and also follow us on **Facebook** and **Twitter** or dip into our **blog**.

Cicerone – the very best guides for exploring the world.

CICERONE

Juniper House, Murley Moss, Oxenholme Road, Kendal, Cumbria LA9 7RL
Tel: 015395 62069 info@cicerone.co.uk
www.cicerone.co.uk